Franco Masetti and Roberto Messa

1001
chess
exercises
for
beginners

**The tactics workbook that explains
the basic concepts, too**

New In Chess 2012

2012 New In Chess
© Le due Torri 2006-2008
English edition published by New In Chess, Alkmaar, The Netherlands
www.newinchess.com
1001 Chess Exercises for Beginners
Translated from *1001 Esercizi per Principianti*
This edition is published by arrangement with Le Due Torri – Chess Department
Store – Italy – www.chess.it

Translation: Richard Jones
Cover design: Volken Beck

ISBN 978-90-5691-397-7

Contents

Introduction

Chess is 99% tactics!

If this celebrated observation is true for the master, how much more so for the beginner and club player.

By far and away, the quickest and most effective way to improve your chess performance is to increase your tactical skill so that at a glance you are able to see the typical mating patterns and material-winning tactical motifs that so often decide a game. There is no doubt that the best way to acquire good tactical vision is to do exercises that teach you to recognise the tactical building blocks that make up every combination. This book focuses on the crucial positions that every chess player must know. It cannot be stressed enough that a knowledge of strategy is of little use if you have not first mastered the fundamentals of tactics.

This book starts with hundreds of essential mating positions that train immediate visual recognition; first there are the easier mate in one or two move exercises; then there are exercises for various crucial tactical motifs that must be mastered by any aspiring chess player; these are followed by more demanding positions where these various motifs are often combined.

While the easier problems can be solved without a chess board, we suggest that for the more difficult ones you set up the positions on a board and try to find the solution as if you were playing a real game. You should therefore not touch or move the pieces before having made your decision, perhaps writing down the possible variations before you check the solutions at the back of the book.

The introductions to each chapter are particularly instructive. It is here that we explain the ideas behind crucial tactical motifs such as double attack, the pin and skewer, as well as pawn promotion, drawing techniques, etc.

This book is intended not only for personal use, but also as a course text book. We have thus consulted leading teachers and masters with extensive training experience working in chess academies and club courses so as to best identify the most productive positions and exercises to use.

Franco Masetti and Roberto Messa

Mate in one

White to move and mate in one
Solutions on page 125

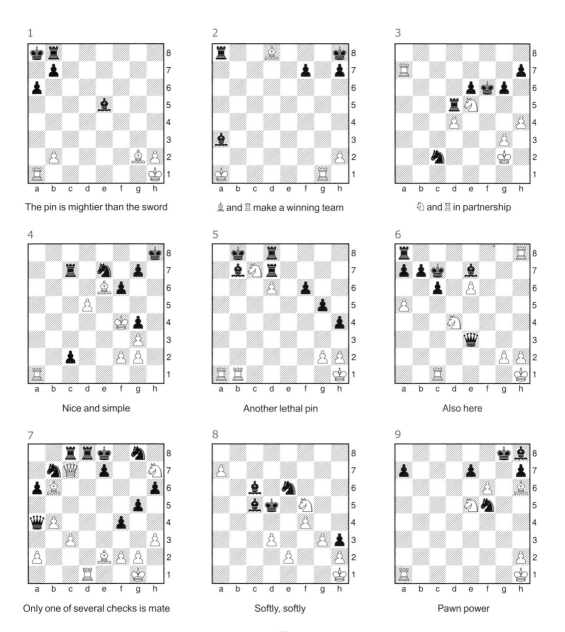

1
The pin is mightier than the sword

2
♗ and ♖ make a winning team

3
♘ and ♖ in partnership

4
Nice and simple

5
Another lethal pin

6
Also here

7
Only one of several checks is mate

8
Softly, softly

9
Pawn power

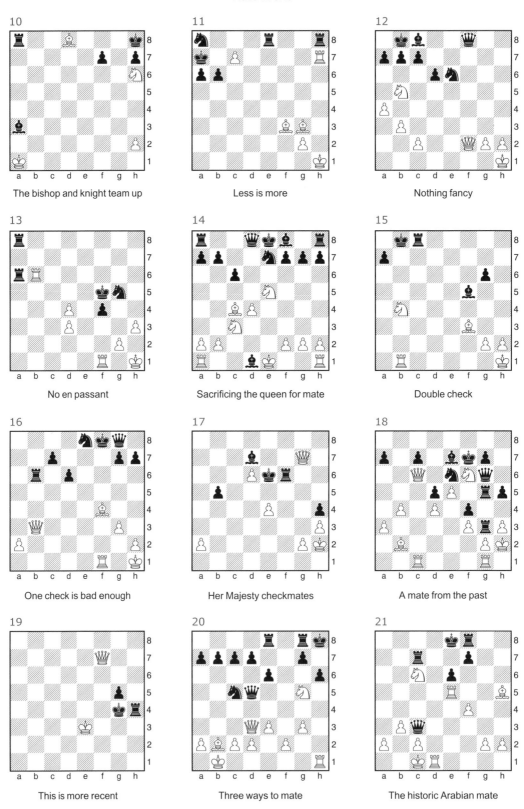

10 — The bishop and knight team up

11 — Less is more

12 — Nothing fancy

13 — No en passant

14 — Sacrificing the queen for mate

15 — Double check

16 — One check is bad enough

17 — Her Majesty checkmates

18 — A mate from the past

19 — This is more recent

20 — Three ways to mate

21 — The historic Arabian mate

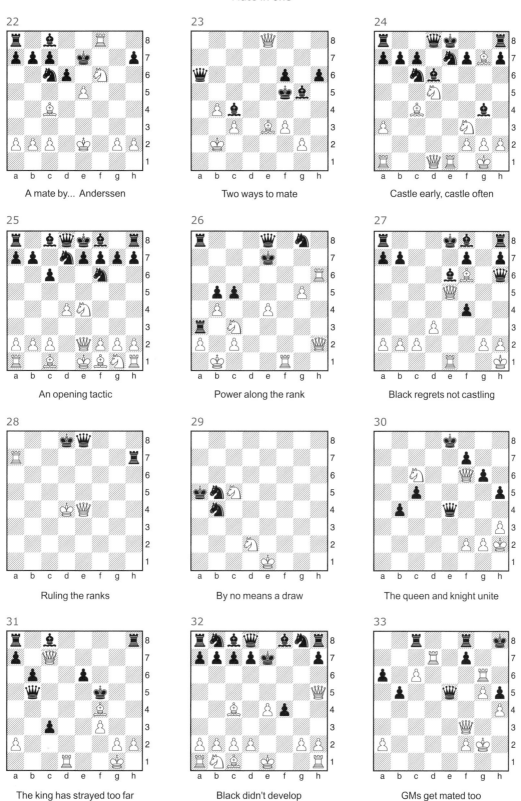

22
A mate by... Anderssen

23
Two ways to mate

24
Castle early, castle often

25
An opening tactic

26
Power along the rank

27
Black regrets not castling

28
Ruling the ranks

29
By no means a draw

30
The queen and knight unite

31
The king has strayed too far

32
Black didn't develop

33
GMs get mated too

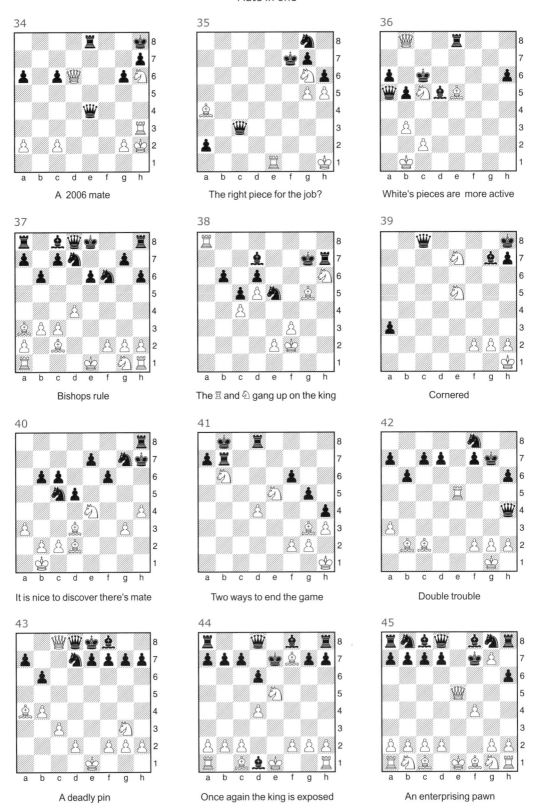

34
A 2006 mate

35
The right piece for the job?

36
White's pieces are more active

37
Bishops rule

38
The ♖ and ♘ gang up on the king

39
Cornered

40
It is nice to discover there's mate

41
Two ways to end the game

42
Double trouble

43
A deadly pin

44
Once again the king is exposed

45
An enterprising pawn

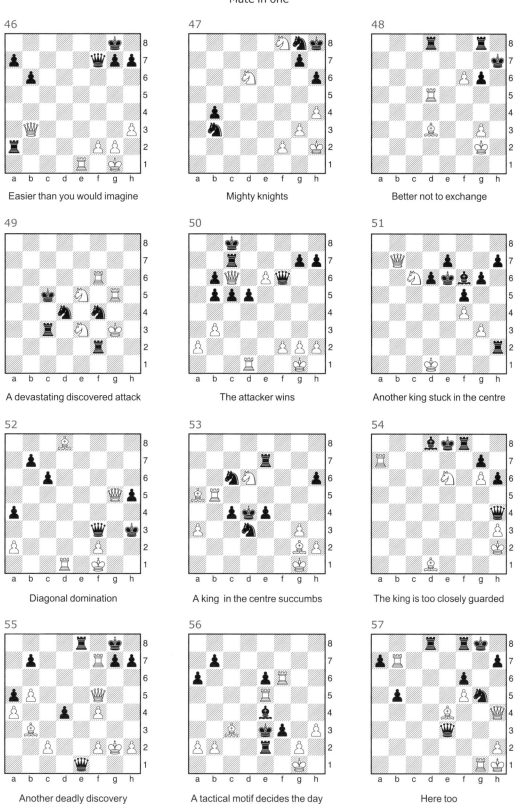

46
Easier than you would imagine

47
Mighty knights

48
Better not to exchange

49
A devastating discovered attack

50
The attacker wins

51
Another king stuck in the centre

52
Diagonal domination

53
A king in the centre succumbs

54
The king is too closely guarded

55
Another deadly discovery

56
A tactical motif decides the day

57
Here too

Mate in two

White to move and mate in two
Solutions on page 125

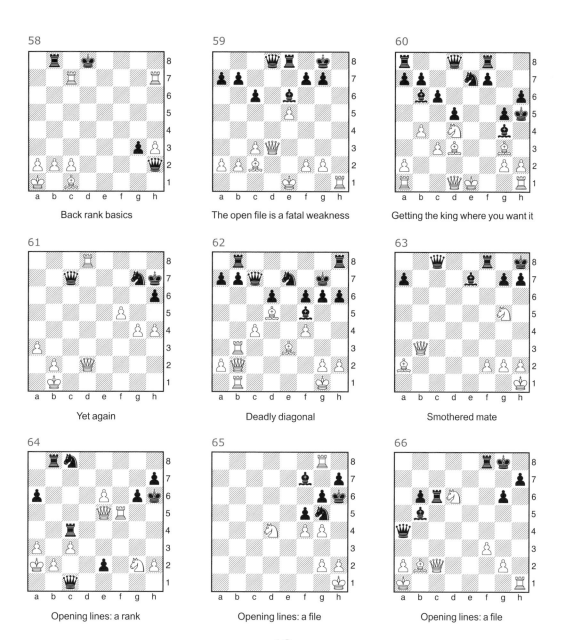

58

Back rank basics

59

The open file is a fatal weakness

60

Getting the king where you want it

61

Yet again

62

Deadly diagonal

63

Smothered mate

64

Opening lines: a rank

65

Opening lines: a file

66

Opening lines: a file

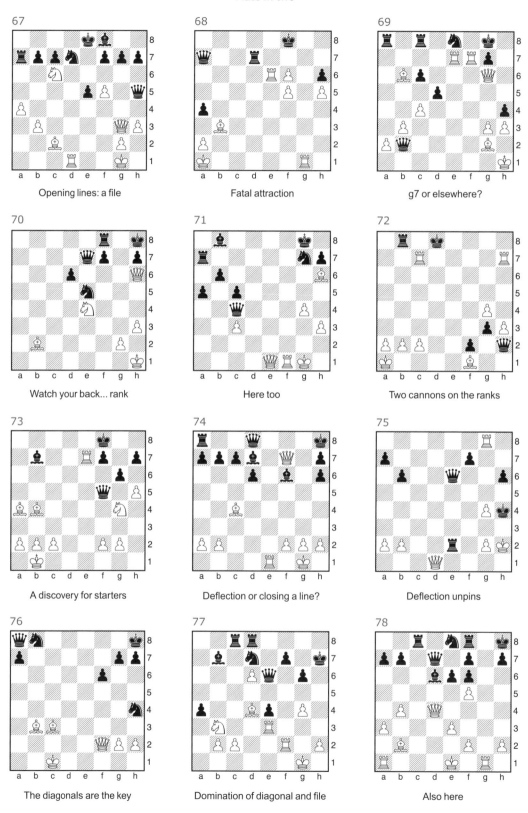

67
Opening lines: a file

68
Fatal attraction

69
g7 or elsewhere?

70
Watch your back... rank

71
Here too

72
Two cannons on the ranks

73
A discovery for starters

74
Deflection or closing a line?

75
Deflection unpins

76
The diagonals are the key

77
Domination of diagonal and file

78
Also here

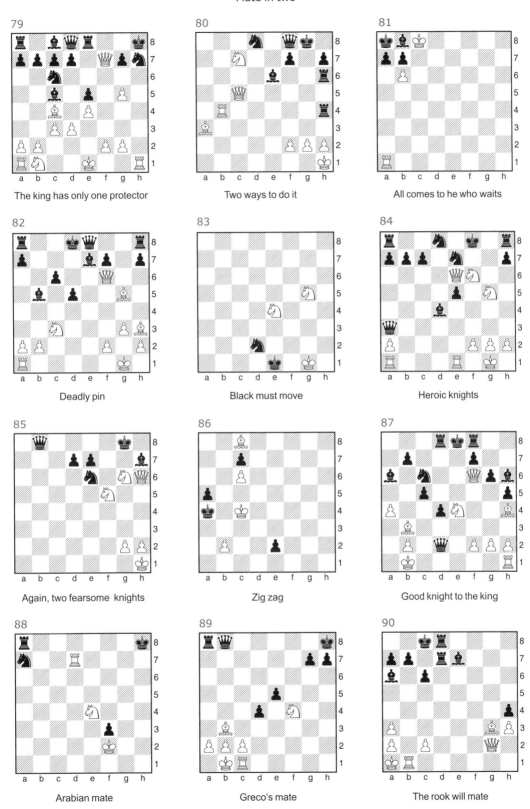

79
The king has only one protector

80
Two ways to do it

81
All comes to he who waits

82
Deadly pin

83
Black must move

84
Heroic knights

85
Again, two fearsome knights

86
Zig zag

87
Good knight to the king

88
Arabian mate

89
Greco's mate

90
The rook will mate

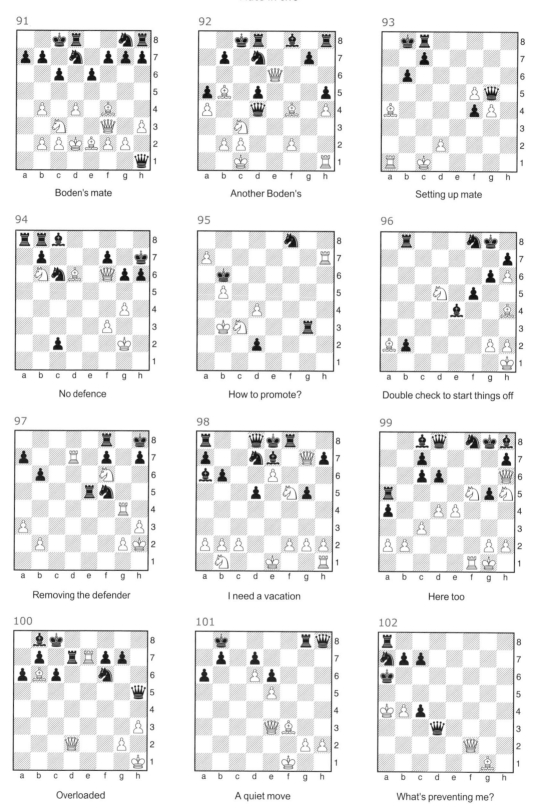

91 Boden's mate

92 Another Boden's

93 Setting up mate

94 No defence

95 How to promote?

96 Double check to start things off

97 Removing the defender

98 I need a vacation

99 Here too

100 Overloaded

101 A quiet move

102 What's preventing me?

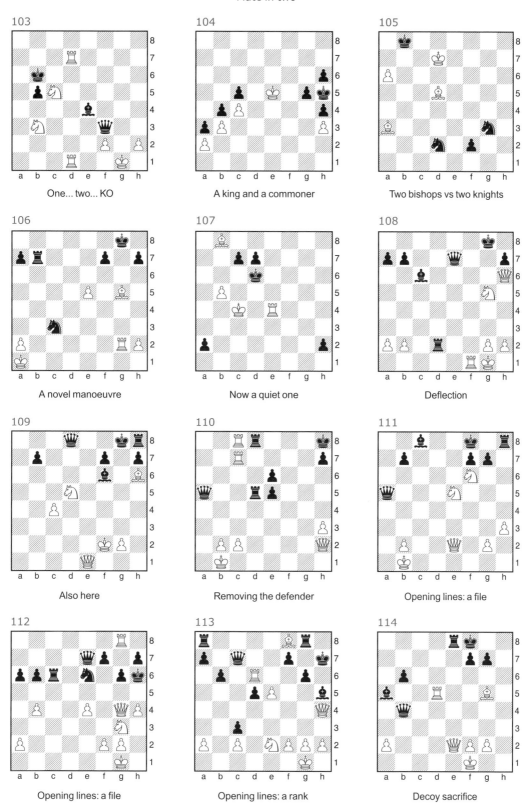

103
One... two... KO

104
A king and a commoner

105
Two bishops vs two knights

106
A novel manoeuvre

107
Now a quiet one

108
Deflection

109
Also here

110
Removing the defender

111
Opening lines: a file

112
Opening lines: a file

113
Opening lines: a rank

114
Decoy sacrifice

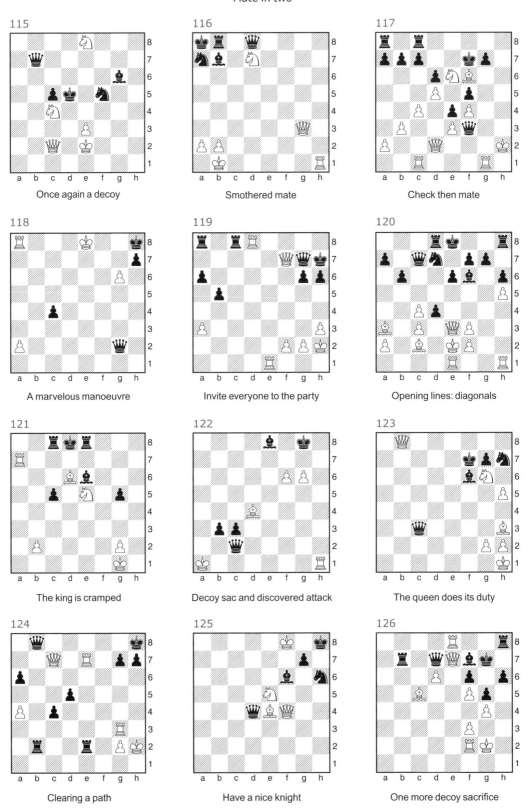

115
Once again a decoy

116
Smothered mate

117
Check then mate

118
A marvelous manoeuvre

119
Invite everyone to the party

120
Opening lines: diagonals

121
The king is cramped

122
Decoy sac and discovered attack

123
The queen does its duty

124
Clearing a path

125
Have a nice knight

126
One more decoy sacrifice

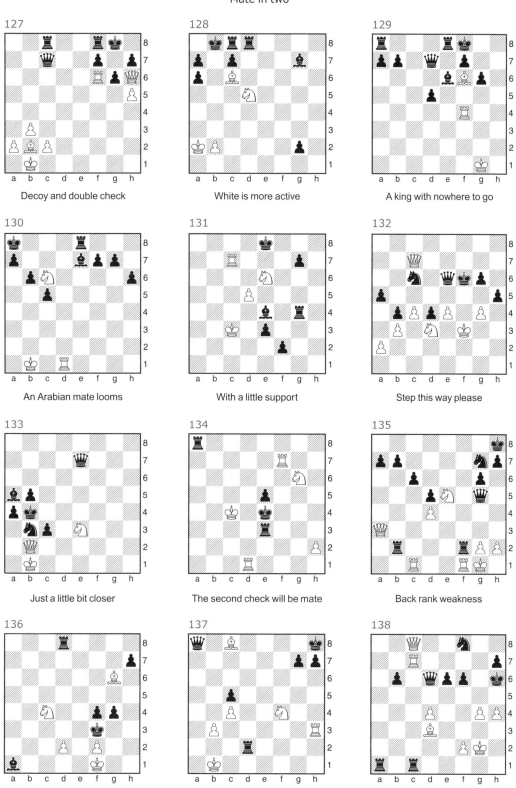

127
Decoy and double check

128
White is more active

129
A king with nowhere to go

130
An Arabian mate looms

131
With a little support

132
Step this way please

133
Just a little bit closer

134
The second check will be mate

135
Back rank weakness

136
d2 or e5?

137
Two checks do the trick

138
Removing the defender

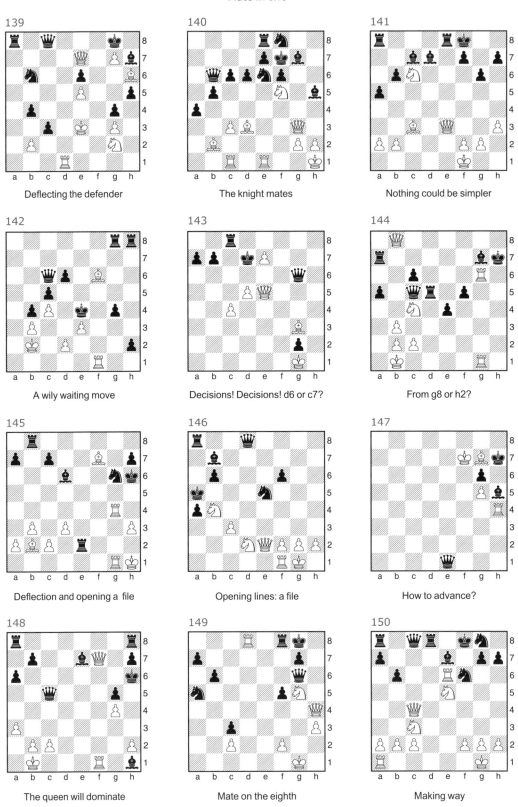

139
Deflecting the defender

140
The knight mates

141
Nothing could be simpler

142
A wily waiting move

143
Decisions! Decisions! d6 or c7?

144
From g8 or h2?

145
Deflection and opening a file

146
Opening lines: a file

147
How to advance?

148
The queen will dominate

149
Mate on the eighth

150
Making way

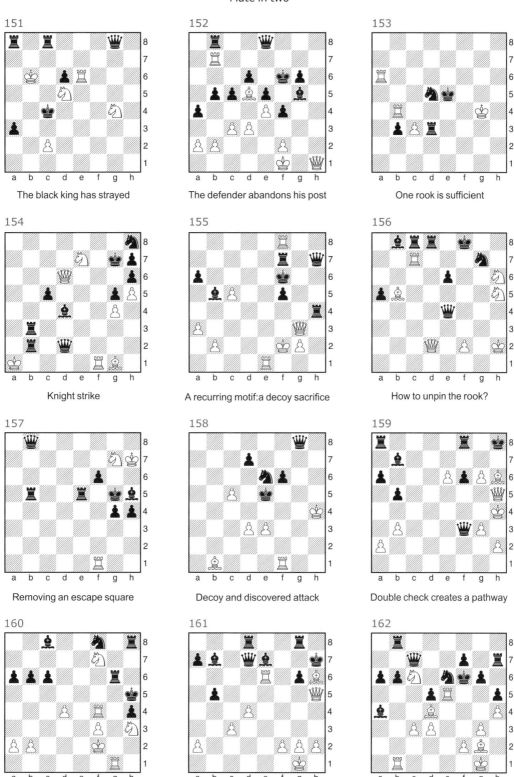

151
The black king has strayed

152
The defender abandons his post

153
One rook is sufficient

154
Knight strike

155
A recurring motif: a decoy sacrifice

156
How to unpin the rook?

157
Removing an escape square

158
Decoy and discovered attack

159
Double check creates a pathway

160
Vacating a square

161
Discovered attack clears the way

162
Discovered attack and decoy

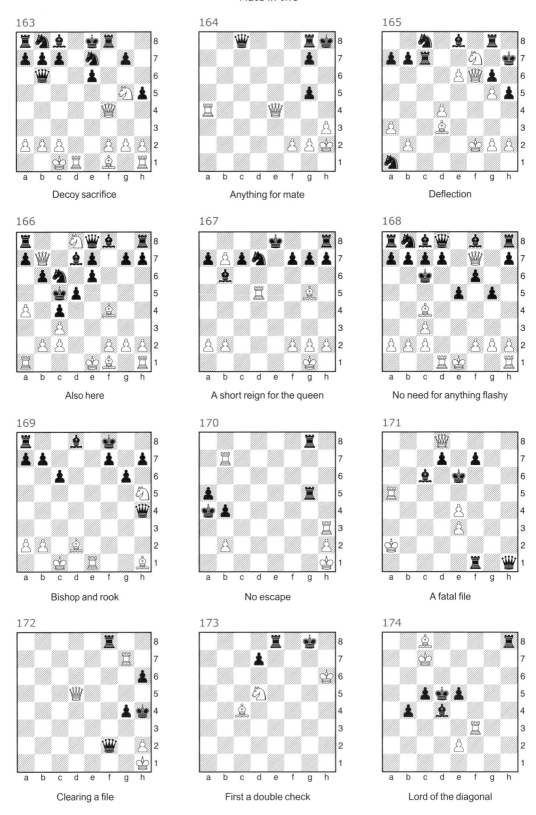

163
Decoy sacrifice

164
Anything for mate

165
Deflection

166
Also here

167
A short reign for the queen

168
No need for anything flashy

169
Bishop and rook

170
No escape

171
A fatal file

172
Clearing a file

173
First a double check

174
Lord of the diagonal

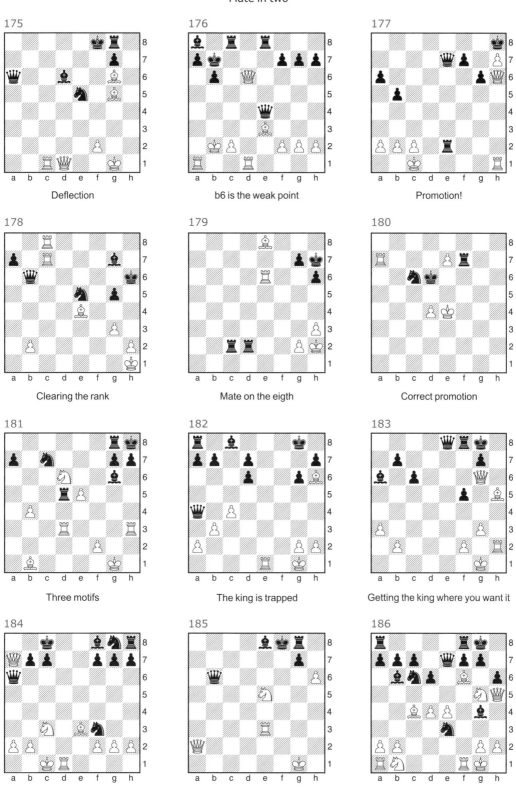

175
Deflection

176
b6 is the weak point

177
Promotion!

178
Clearing the rank

179
Mate on the eigth

180
Correct promotion

181
Three motifs

182
The king is trapped

183
Getting the king where you want it

184
Mate on the back rank

185
The knight delivers

186
No defence

The missing piece!

In these valuable exercises you have to place a piece on the board so as to create checkmate or a winning position. These exercises are more than just good fun; they improve pattern recognition, visualisation and creativity as well.

Solutions on page 127

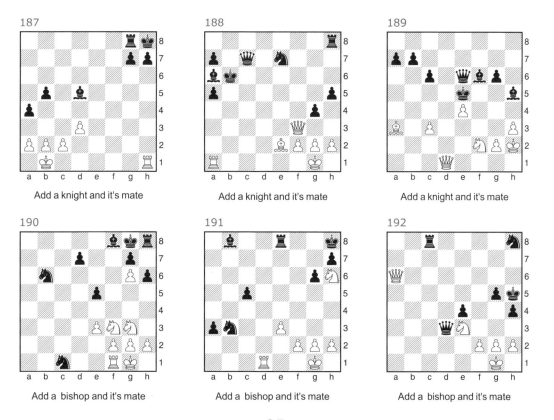

187
Add a knight and it's mate

188
Add a knight and it's mate

189
Add a knight and it's mate

190
Add a bishop and it's mate

191
Add a bishop and it's mate

192
Add a bishop and it's mate

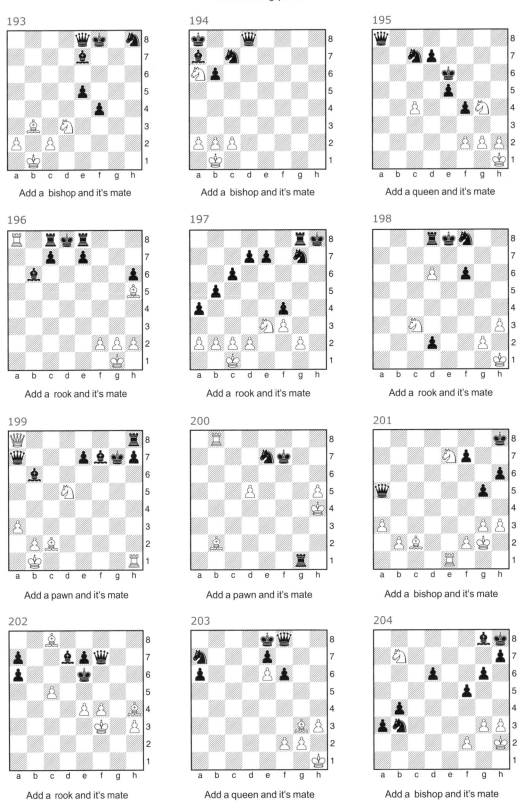

193
Add a bishop and it's mate

194
Add a bishop and it's mate

195
Add a queen and it's mate

196
Add a rook and it's mate

197
Add a rook and it's mate

198
Add a rook and it's mate

199
Add a pawn and it's mate

200
Add a pawn and it's mate

201
Add a bishop and it's mate

202
Add a rook and it's mate

203
Add a queen and it's mate

204
Add a bishop and it's mate

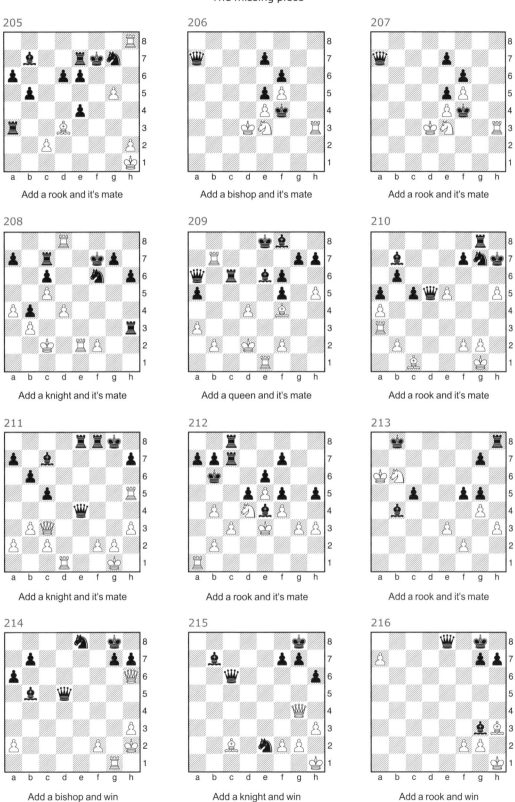

205
Add a rook and it's mate

206
Add a bishop and it's mate

207
Add a rook and it's mate

208
Add a knight and it's mate

209
Add a queen and it's mate

210
Add a rook and it's mate

211
Add a knight and it's mate

212
Add a rook and it's mate

213
Add a rook and it's mate

214
Add a bishop and win

215
Add a knight and win

216
Add a rook and win

Double attack

White to move
Solutions on page 127

So far we have looked at lots and lots of mating positions. This is clearly logical as delivering checkmate is the objective of the game. However, checkmate is much easier to achieve when we have an advantage in material, namely more pieces.

Combinations of tactical motifs that force a gain in material occur in virtually every game, and the most important of these motifs are based on some kind of double attack .

However, double attack is most commonly used to describe a position in which one piece attacks two undefended pieces simultaneously and only one of those threatened pieces is able to save itself. It goes without saying that it is rare that in a single move one's opponent can save or protect two attacked pieces. Let's look at an example.

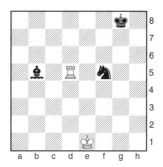

White has just played 1. ♖d5, creating a double attack on the bishop and knight. One of the two pieces will be captured on the next move.

We have already noted that a double attack is very often impossible to meet. However, this is not always the case; in certain positions a fleeing piece can protect another.

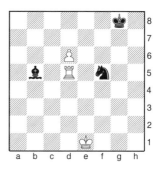

In this position, which is almost identical to the preceding one, Black can save both pieces with the simple move 1... ♗d7.

There is also the 'double threat' motif, which arises when at least one of our attacks does not involve the threat of material gain, but instead another type of threat such as checkmate.

29

In this position White plays 1. ♕e4!, simultaneously threatening checkmate with 2. ♕xh7 and the capture of the rook on a8. Black has no choice but to defend his king, leaving the poor rook to its fate.

In the following example the position of the white king allows a most unpleasant surprise! Black has the luxury of choosing between two moves that not only save both his threatened pieces, but which also win the white rook.

In reply to White's double attack, Black can play either 1... ♗c6, 'pinning' the rook to the king, or launch his own double attack with 1... ♘e3+!

This example teaches us that before making a double attack we have to make sure that our opponent does not have tactical resources of his own.

All the pieces can create a double attack, including the king and the pawn. Perhaps the most dangerous is the knight; its unusual way of moving allows it to attack two pieces without being attacked itself and renders its movements more visually difficult to anticipate!

A double attack by a pawn or a knight is usually called a 'fork'.

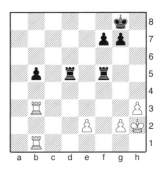

In this position White will win one of the two rooks by playing 1. e4.
A classic pawn fork!

As mentioned before, a double attack in the broadest sense is central to most of the tactical motifs discussed in the following chapters; for example, a discovery is no more than a sophisticated form of double attack.

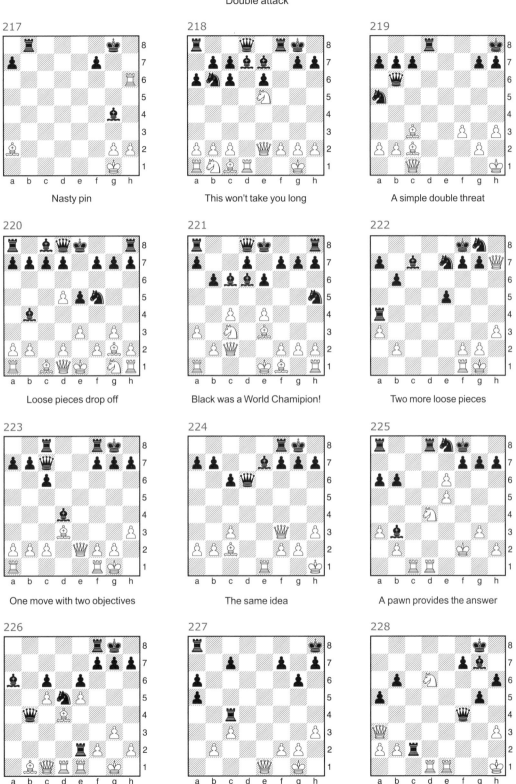

217
Nasty pin

218
This won't take you long

219
A simple double threat

220
Loose pieces drop off

221
Black was a World Champion!

222
Two more loose pieces

223
One move with two objectives

224
The same idea

225
A pawn provides the answer

226
Simple chess

227
Check then a double attack

228
This is trickier

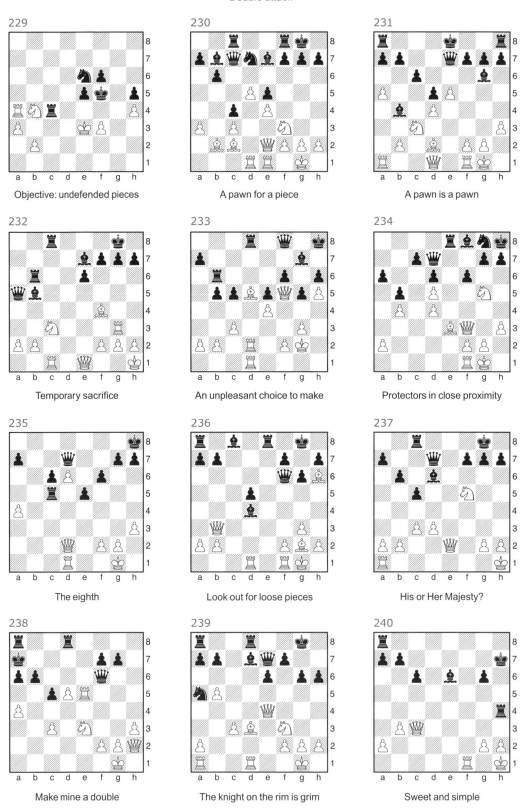

229
Objective: undefined pieces

230
A pawn for a piece

231
A pawn is a pawn

232
Temporary sacrifice

233
An unpleasant choice to make

234
Protectors in close proximity

235
The eighth

236
Look out for loose pieces

237
His or Her Majesty?

238
Make mine a double

239
The knight on the rim is grim

240
Sweet and simple

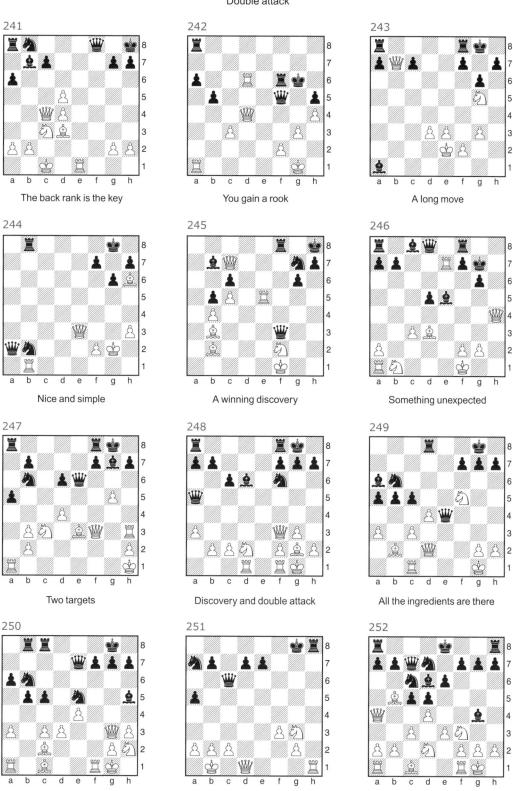

Double attack

241
The back rank is the key

242
You gain a rook

243
A long move

244
Nice and simple

245
A winning discovery

246
Something unexpected

247
Two targets

248
Discovery and double attack

249
All the ingredients are there

250
Fifth rank

251
If only the king were...

252
Two bishops in danger

33

Discovered attack

White to move
Solutions on page 128

A discovered attack is a form of double attack where one piece moves to attack another, unmasking an attack by a second piece.

In the above position, the knight can jump to d4, unleashing an attack on the black queen. Black is forced to choose the lesser of two evils, and accept the loss of the bishop on f5.

As always, things do not necessarily work out as we plan, and we must always check carefully that our opponent does not surprise us with an 'acrobatic' defence.

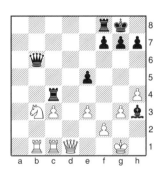

In the example above White can play 1. ♘d2, with a discovered attack that threatens both queen and rook. However, the strong reply of 1... ♕c6! solves Black's problems; thanks to the threat of mate on g2, Black has sufficient time to save the rook, for example: 2. e4 ♖xc3.

Yet another example of how time and geometry are the fundamental building blocks of chess tactics.

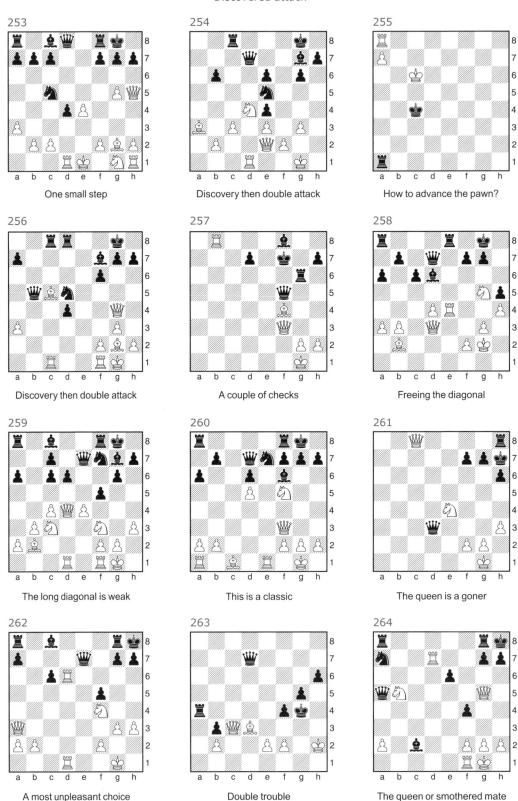

253
One small step

254
Discovery then double attack

255
How to advance the pawn?

256
Discovery then double attack

257
A couple of checks

258
Freeing the diagonal

259
The long diagonal is weak

260
This is a classic

261
The queen is a goner

262
A most unpleasant choice

263
Double trouble

264
The queen or smothered mate

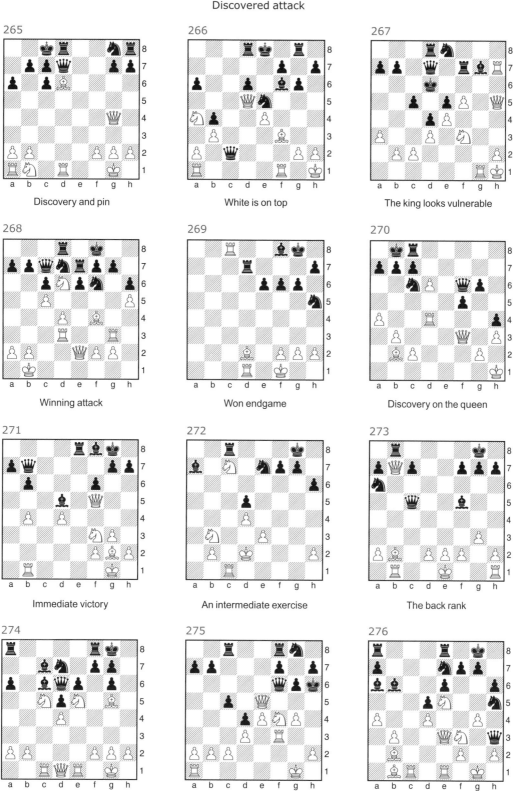

265
Discovery and pin

266
White is on top

267
The king looks vulnerable

268
Winning attack

269
Won endgame

270
Discovery on the queen

271
Immediate victory

272
An intermediate exercise

273
The back rank

274
Black's pieces are badly placed

275
An elegant double threat

276
Mating attack

Discovered check

A discovered check occurs when the target of the unmasked piece in a discovered attack is none other than His Majesty himself. As a result they are particulary dangerous.

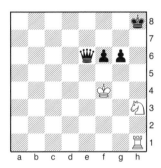

White plays 1. ♘g5+ with a discovered check, picking up the queen on the next move.

The following examples will give you a even better idea of the devastating power of a discovered check .

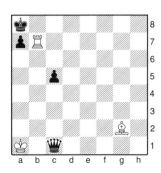

In defending his king, White unleashes a discovered check: 1. ♖b1! ... which is indeed checkmate!

The last example is as instructive as it is entertaining.

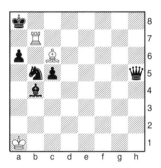

1. ♖xb5+ ♚a7 2. ♖b7+ ♚a8

The poor black king is forced back to the critical square.

3. ♖xb4+ ♚a7 4. ♖b7+ ♚a8 5. ♖h7+ ♚b8 6. ♖xh5

This series of discovered checks concludes with the capture of a good three pieces.

This nightmare form of déjà vu is called a 'windmill'. Though infrequent, it is one of the most delightful of all tactical motifs.

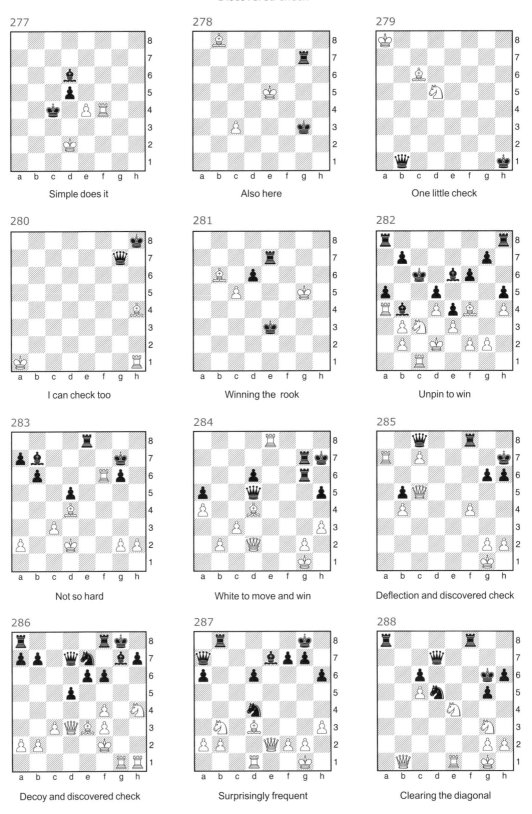

277
Simple does it

278
Also here

279
One little check

280
I can check too

281
Winning the rook

282
Unpin to win

283
Not so hard

284
White to move and win

285
Deflection and discovered check

286
Decoy and discovered check

287
Surprisingly frequent

288
Clearing the diagonal

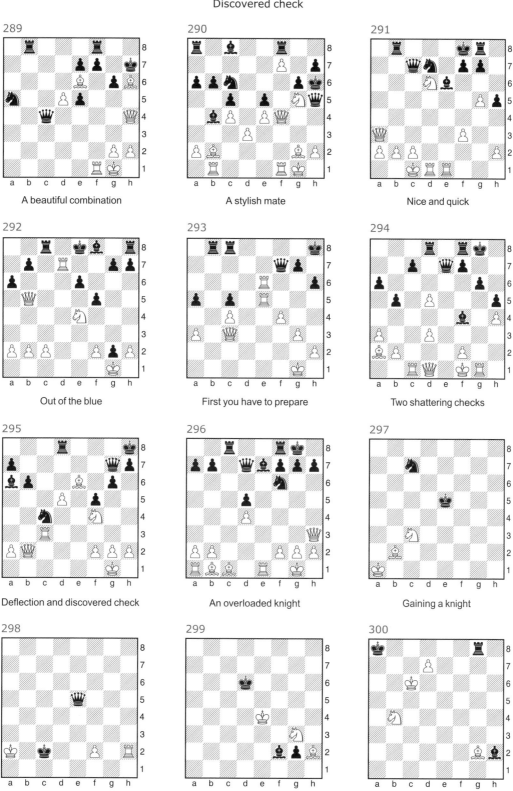

289
A beautiful combination

290
A stylish mate

291
Nice and quick

292
Out of the blue

293
First you have to prepare

294
Two shattering checks

295
Deflection and discovered check

296
An overloaded knight

297
Gaining a knight

298
How to prevent mate?

299
Turning the corner

300
Mate in 3 to finish things off

Double check

White to move
Solutions on page 129

Double check is a type of discovered check where one piece moves to give check and uncovers another piece that also attacks the king. Needless to say this is a bombshell and two out of the three possible ways of defending the king no longer apply: it is not possible to interpose with a piece, as check arrives from two directions; you cannot capture the checking piece because there are two of them. The only remaining hope is to move the king to a safe square, presuming there is one ...

controlled by the two attacking pieces. It is amusing to note that both the checking pieces are hanging, but because of the power of a double check they are immune from capture.

The following diagram shows the superiority of a double check compared to a normal discovered check.

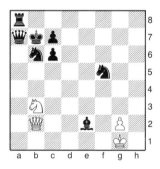

Black, with an enormous material advantage, hopes to finish things off immediately with 1... ♘c4+?. This would be a grave error, as White can reply with a double check: 2. ♘c5+ ♚c8 (Black cannot capture either the queen on b2 or the knight on c5 due to the double check) 3. ♕h8#

In the above position White ends the game with the killing 1. ♗c6#. The king's two escape squares are

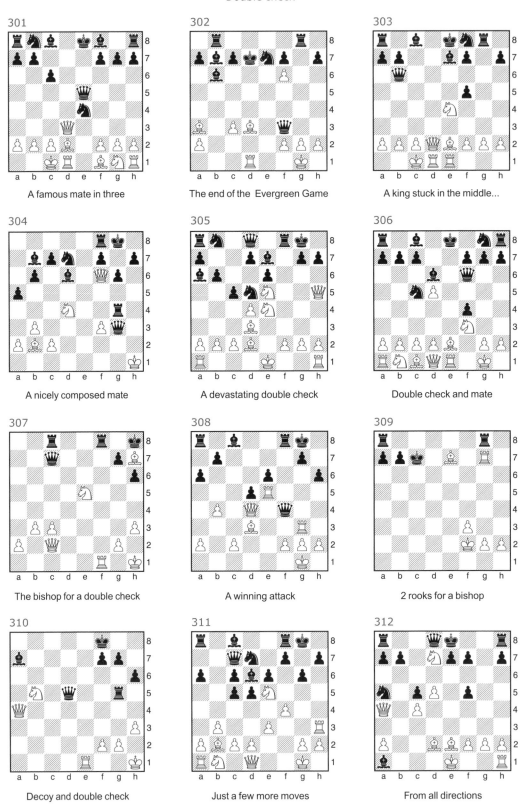

301
A famous mate in three

302
The end of the Evergreen Game

303
A king stuck in the middle...

304
A nicely composed mate

305
A devastating double check

306
Double check and mate

307
The bishop for a double check

308
A winning attack

309
2 rooks for a bishop

310
Decoy and double check

311
Just a few more moves

312
From all directions

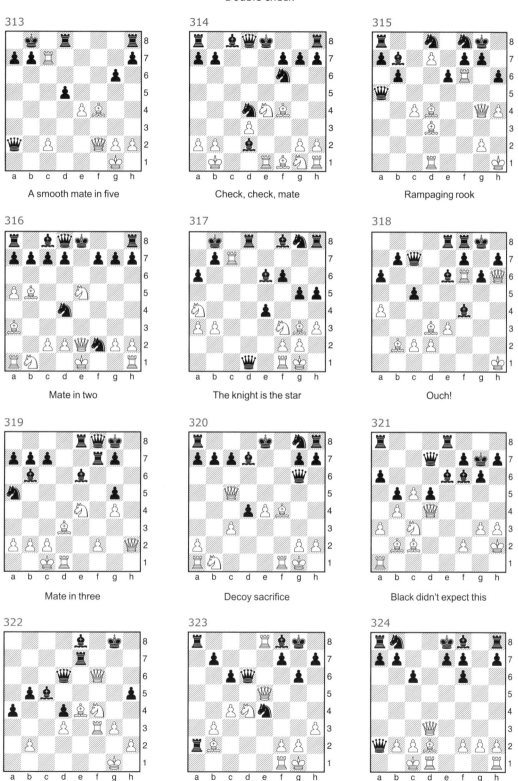

313
A smooth mate in five

314
Check, check, mate

315
Rampaging rook

316
Mate in two

317
The knight is the star

318
Ouch!

319
Mate in three

320
Decoy sacrifice

321
Black didn't expect this

322
F-file

323
Seen before... but improved

324
Black threatens mate on a1

Pin

White to move
Solutions on page 129

When a piece is on the same line of attack as its king, it cannot move. It is 'pinned'. In the following position the black rook is pinned by the white bishop and cannot avoid capture.

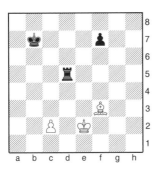

Black can try to limit the loss of material by playing 1... ♔c6, after which White should not be hasty: if he contents himself with winning the exchange with 2. ♗xd5+? ♔xd5 he will achieve no more than a draw; whereas if he piles on the pressure with 2. c4!, he will win the rook for nothing on the following move. The rook cannot escape because of the paralysing pin.

The pin is a very common tactical motif that can often lead to a gain in material or mate itself.

In the following position the 'protection' of the king by Black's pieces is an optical illusion.

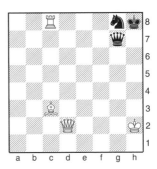

However, their presence makes seeing the mating move 1. ♕h6# much more difficult.

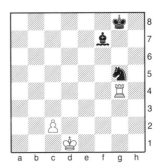

As with all tactical ideas it is always necessary to anticipate your opponent's reply. In the example above, White has just played 1. ♖g4, taking advantage of the pin to win the knight, but after 1. ♗h5, White's smile will become a frown as he realises his rook is now itself pinned, with a won game for Black!

When a piece is pinned to the king, we have an absolute pin. If the piece is pinned to any other piece, this is called a relative pin, as it is always possible that it may be opportune for the pinned piece to move and leave the formerly shielded piece to its fate.

In this well known opening variation, it would appear that White can win the d pawn, exploiting the fact that the knight on f6 is pinned to the queen. In fact, 1. ♘xd5? is a blunder, as Black can reply 1... ♘xd5!; and after 2. ♗xd8 ♗b4+! 3. ♕d2 ♗xd2+ 4. ♔xd2 ♔xd8, White finds himself down a piece.

Even with an absolute pin, there are times when the defender can free himself from what appears to be a devastating pin.

In the above position the knight on c6 is pinned to the king by the white bishop and at the same time it is attacked by the pawn on d5.

At first glance the knight looks doomed. However, Black has a typical unpinning manoeuvre at his disposal: 1... a6! 2. ♗a4 (the only move that maintains White's threat; the alternatives 2. ♗xc6+ bxc6 and 2. dxc6 axb5 gain nothing) 2... b5!.

By continuing to harass the white bishop, Black has neutralised the pin; after 3. dxc6 bxa4 or 3. ♗b3 ♘a5 etc, the position remains balanced.

This example teaches us that in the opening a pinned knight on c6 or f6 (c3 or f3 for White) is not something to be overly afraid of. It is only in some cases that it is advisable to prevent the pin with h6 or a6; in many others the prophylactic pawn move is a useless waste of time that creates a potential target.

Often, Black can safely respond to the pinning move ♗g5 by playing ♗e7; otherwise, but only after the arrival of the bishop, Black may choose to 'put the question' to White's bishop with h6.

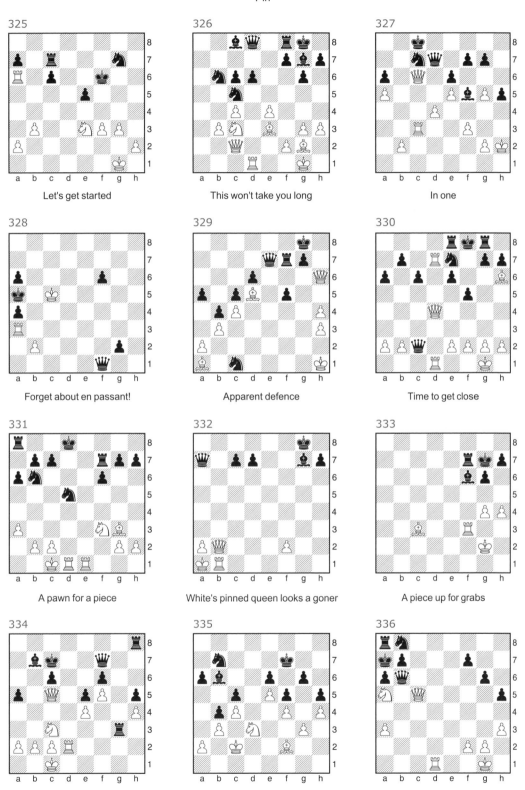

325
Let's get started

326
This won't take you long

327
In one

328
Forget about en passant!

329
Apparent defence

330
Time to get close

331
A pawn for a piece

332
White's pinned queen looks a goner

333
A piece up for grabs

334
The pin provides a fork

335
Loose pieces...

336
Absolute and relative

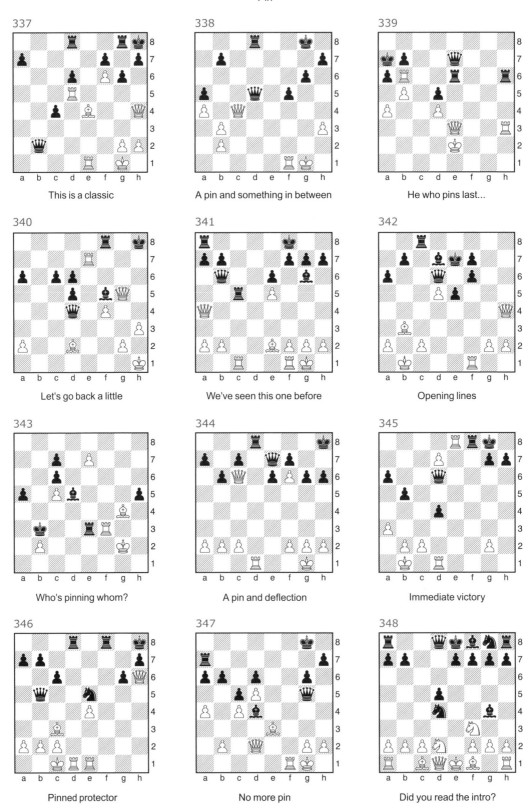

337 This is a classic

338 A pin and something in between

339 He who pins last...

340 Let's go back a little

341 We've seen this one before

342 Opening lines

343 Who's pinning whom?

344 A pin and deflection

345 Immediate victory

346 Pinned protector

347 No more pin

348 Did you read the intro?

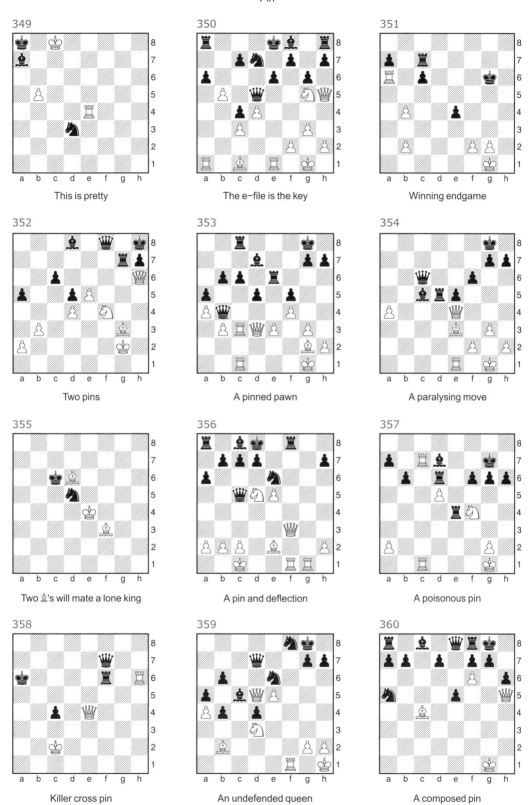

349

This is pretty

350

The e-file is the key

351

Winning endgame

352

Two pins

353

A pinned pawn

354

A paralysing move

355

Two ♗'s will mate a lone king

356

A pin and deflection

357

A poisonous pin

358

Killer cross pin

359

An undefended queen

360

A composed pin

Skewer

White to move
Solutions on page 130

On closer examination a skewer is also a double attack. This is due its x-ray nature; when a more valuable piece moves out of the way of an attack, the attack continues through to a less valuable one. Only long-range pieces can skewer, namely the queen, rook and bishop. King and knight skewers do not exist.

As always, a diagram is worth a thousand words.

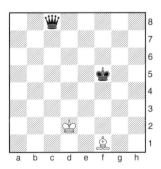

By playing 1. ♗h3+, White wins the queen.

As mentioned before, our enthusiasm for a possible tactical opportunity can blind us to a possible defence by our adversary.

The skewer is no exception.

White skewers the king with 1. ♗g2+, but if Black were to play the prudent defence 1... ♔c4, capturing the rook on b7 would be a fatal error. Instead, White must make a move to parry the threat of 2...♖a5#. This gives Black time to save the rook, with a winning material and positional advantage. Never underestimate your opponent's defensive resources!

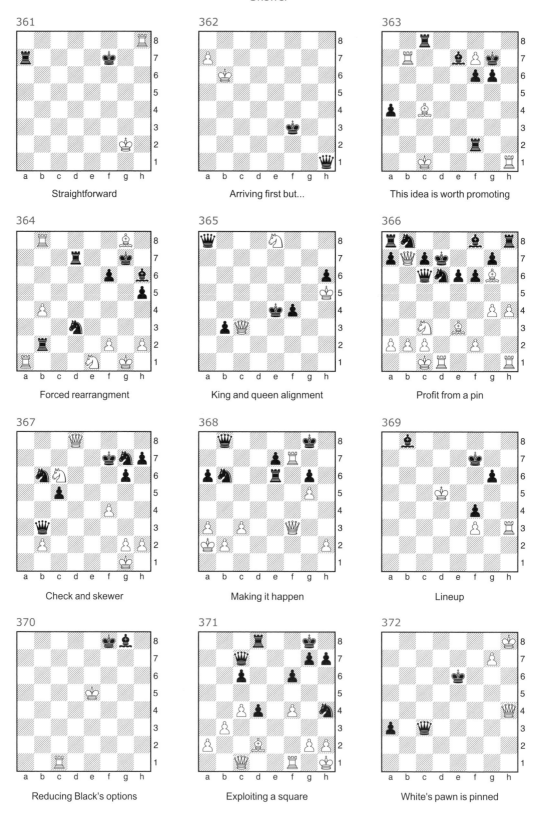

361
Straightforward

362
Arriving first but...

363
This idea is worth promoting

364
Forced rearrangment

365
King and queen alignment

366
Profit from a pin

367
Check and skewer

368
Making it happen

369
Lineup

370
Reducing Black's options

371
Exploiting a square

372
White's pawn is pinned

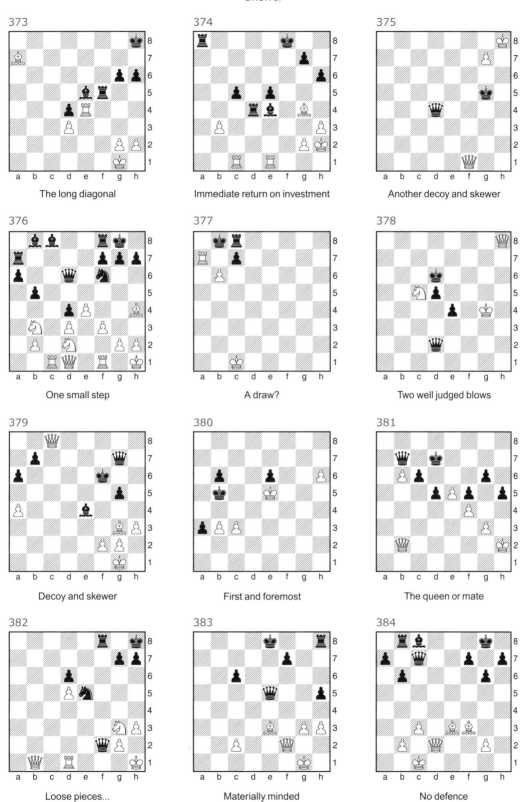

373
The long diagonal

374
Immediate return on investment

375
Another decoy and skewer

376
One small step

377
A draw?

378
Two well judged blows

379
Decoy and skewer

380
First and foremost

381
The queen or mate

382
Loose pieces...

383
Materially minded

384
No defence

Deflection

White to move
Solutions on page 131

Deflection is a tactical motif whose objective is to force a piece away from the defence of another piece or a key square.

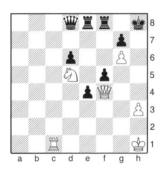

The black queen guards the h4 square, which is a role of vital importance as from this square the white queen can force checkmate. By making a deflection sacrifice, White can put his queen on this key square: 1. Rc8! Qxc8 (the black queen cannot continue to guard h4, as the squares e7, f6 and g5 are all under White's control) 2. Qh4+ Kg8 3. Qh7#

Deflection, like all tactical motifs, can be combined with other elements, as illustrated in the following position.

With the spectacular 1. Re8!!, White initiates a combination that includes deflection and a pin; Black has no choice but to part with his rook to avoid checkmate.

The plight of the black queen is miserable: if 1... Qb6, there is 2. Qg7# (the g8 R is pinned); 1... Qc7 will be met by 2. Qf6+ followed by mate; after1... Qd4 (the only move that parries all the mating threats, but leaves the b8R undefended), there is 2. R3xg8+ Bxg8 3. Rxb8 and White has a decisive advantage: the double attack 3... Qe5+ fails because of 4. f4 (4... Qxb8 is answered by 5. Qf6#).

The chess term for describing a piece that has more defensive tasks than it can cope with is 'overloaded'.

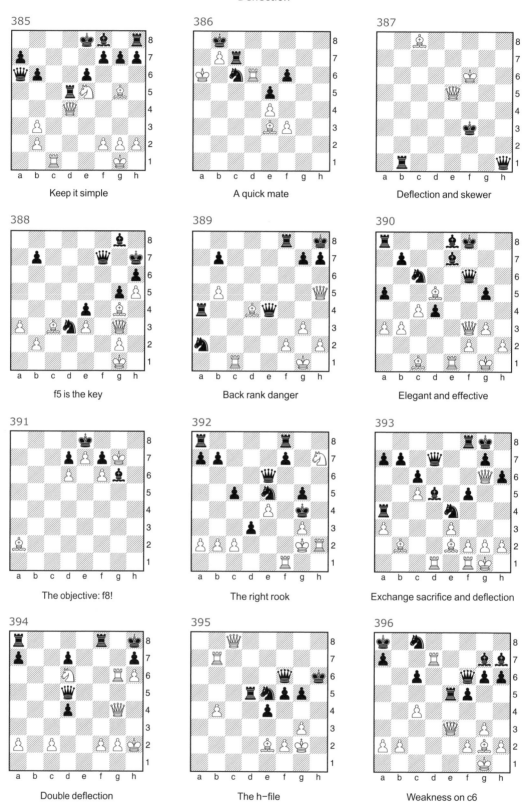

385
Keep it simple

386
A quick mate

387
Deflection and skewer

388
f5 is the key

389
Back rank danger

390
Elegant and effective

391
The objective: f8!

392
The right rook

393
Exchange sacrifice and deflection

394
Double deflection

395
The h-file

396
Weakness on c6

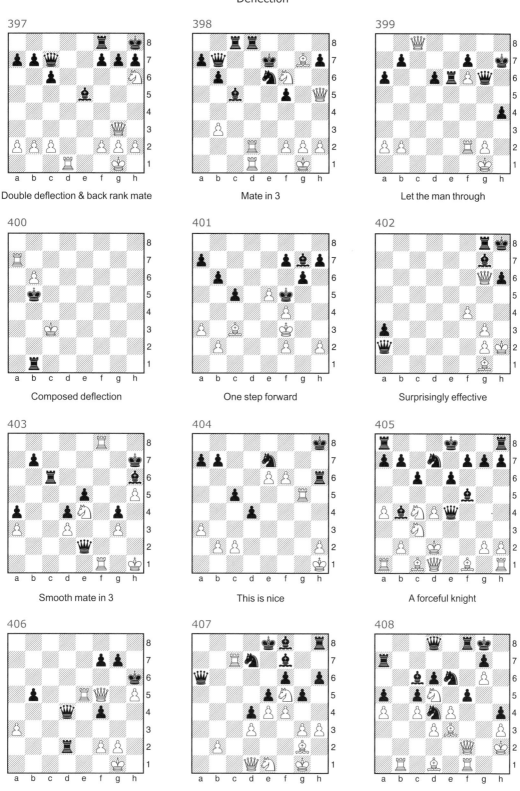

397
Double deflection & back rank mate

398
Mate in 3

399
Let the man through

400
Composed deflection

401
One step forward

402
Surprisingly effective

403
Smooth mate in 3

404
This is nice

405
A forceful knight

406
A king has walked into danger

407
The black queen is overloaded

408
h4 holds the answer

Decoy sacrifice

White to play
Solutions on page 131

We should always be on the lookout for a sacrifice that draws an opponent's piece onto a critical square. A decoy sacrifice's objective could be to deliver checkmate or to win material.

Let's look at a combination that finishes with mate; the first step is an initial sacrifice to clear the g6 square; then a decoy sacrifice to drag the black king onto f8 and then the bishop and rook quickly finish off the defenceless king.

1. ♘f6+! gxf6 (not accepting the sacrifice leads to immediate mate) 2. ♕f8+! (the decoy sacrifice) 2... ♔xf8 3. ♗h6+ ♔g8 4. ♖e8#

In the following positions the decoy sacrifices result in a gain in material; As always, in the following two examples the decoy sacrifice is followed by another tactical motif; in our first example it is a fork, in the second a pin.

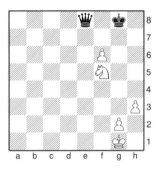

1. f7+! (a pawn fork that forces either the king or queen onto f7, allowing a devastating knight fork) 1... ♕xf7 2. ♘h6+; otherwise 1... ♔xf7 2. ♘d6+ and White wins easily.

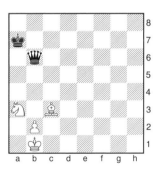

1. ♗d4 ♕xd4 (the pinned queen cannot escape its fate) 2. ♘b5+ and White wins.

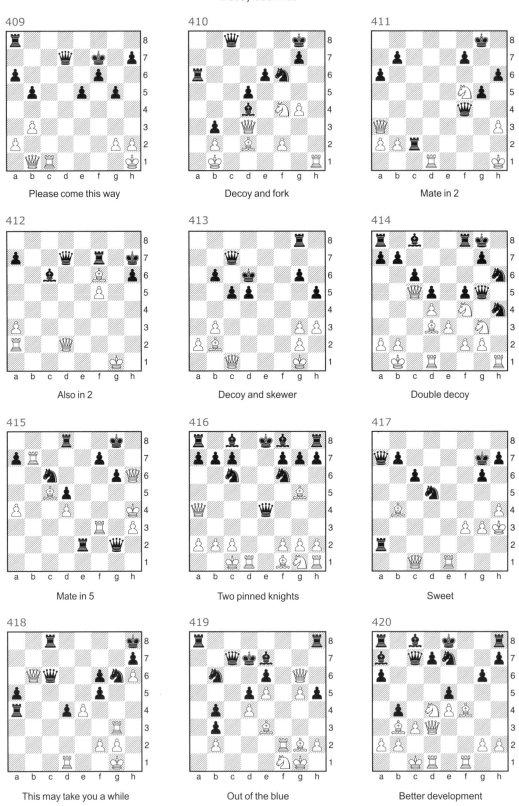

409

Please come this way

410

Decoy and fork

411

Mate in 2

412

Also in 2

413

Decoy and skewer

414

Double decoy

415

Mate in 5

416

Two pinned knights

417

Sweet

418

This may take you a while

419

Out of the blue

420

Better development

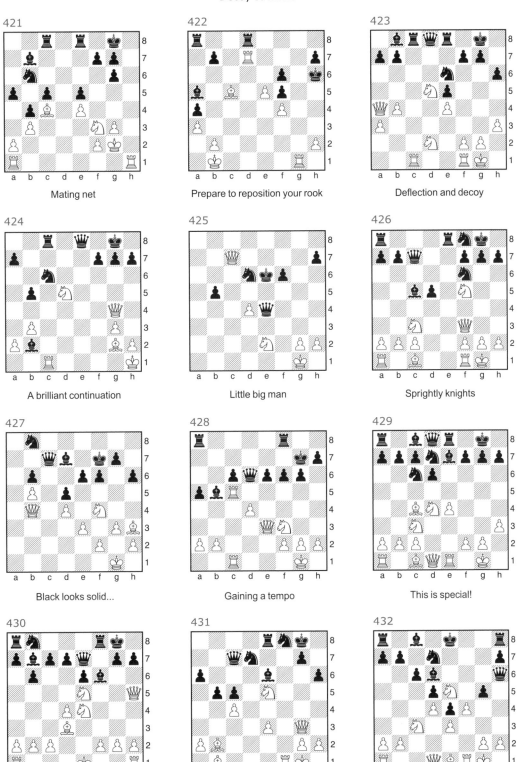

421
Mating net

422
Prepare to reposition your rook

423
Deflection and decoy

424
A brilliant continuation

425
Little big man

426
Sprightly knights

427
Black looks solid...

428
Gaining a tempo

429
This is special!

430
The most famous decoy sacrifice

431
Spectacular sacrifice

432
Get him where you want him

Promotion

White to move
Solutions on page 132

The march a pawn makes to promote, either to become a queen or another piece, involves a wide variety of positions of tactical interest. These usually occur in the endgame, when the fewer pieces on the board often have difficulty stopping the progress of an ambitious pawn; however, promotion related tactics can also occur much earlier in the game.

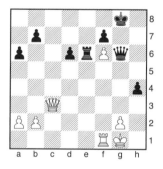

In this position White can play a combination so that his advanced pawn can promote: 1. ♕c8+ ♔h7 2. ♕xe6! fxe6 3. f7 h3 (Black plays his last card; indeed, if White now continues with 4. f8=♕??, there is mate from h2); instead, 4.f8=♘+! ♔g7 5. ♘xg6 ♔xg6 and White wins.

Though promoting to a knight is rare, it occurs more than one would imagine.

In the endgame, tactics related to promotion many times involve a pawn being 'outside the square', thus beyond the king's reach.

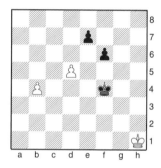

In the above position, for example, the king is still in the square of the b4 pawn (i.e. the square whose corners are b4, b8, f4 and f8). However, White can create an obstacle on the black king's path: 1. d6! exd6 2. b5 ♔e5 3. b6 and no matter what Black plays 4. b7 is unstoppable and White wins.

White's pawn sacrifice blocks the f4-b8 diagonal and the black king was unable to remain within the square of the passed pawn as it marched towards promotion.

Even when there are still pieces in play, the rule of the square may create surprises, as with the following game,

65

in which former World Champion Mikhail Tal was characteristically quick to exploit a tactical opportunity.

White had to deal with the threat of 1... h2 followed by 2... ♕e4+ and then promotion on h1. He thus played 1. ♕f3?, thinking that after an exchange of queens his king would still be within the square of the h3 pawn.

However, Tal saw deeper than that and played 1... ♕xf3+!; and after 2. ♔xf3 ♘e3!, White had no choice but to resign, as the knight move makes the prevention of 3... h2 and subsequent promotion impossible.

Pawn promotion can involve many different tactical motifs. In the following position White uses the threat of promotion to win a rook by means of a skewer.

Things get started with a sacrifice: 1. b6! cxb6 (forced; otherwise White

wins with 2. b7) 2. a7! ♖xa7 (again necessary to prevent 3. a8=♕) 3. ♖g7+ followed by 4. ♖xa7.

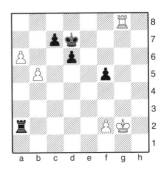

The last example shows the themes of pawn promotion and deflection in tandem.

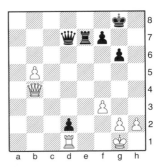

The promotion of Black's passed pawn seems to have been successfuly prevented by White. Then came the rude shock of 1... ♖e1+! 2. ♖xe1 ♕d4+! (deflecting the queen from the b4-e1 diagonal) 3. ♕xd4 dxe1=♕#

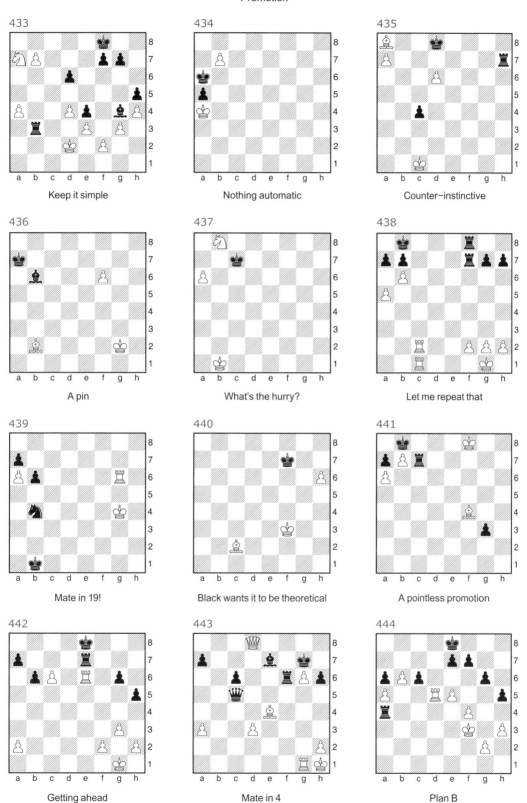

433

Keep it simple

434

Nothing automatic

435

Counter-instinctive

436

A pin

437

What's the hurry?

438

Let me repeat that

439

Mate in 19!

440

Black wants it to be theoretical

441

A pointless promotion

442

Getting ahead

443

Mate in 4

444

Plan B

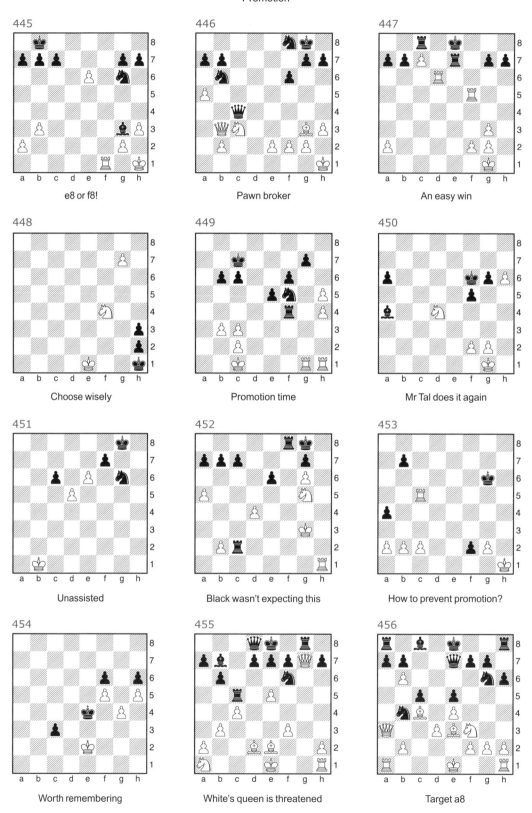

445
e8 or f8!

446
Pawn broker

447
An easy win

448
Choose wisely

449
Promotion time

450
Mr Tal does it again

451
Unassisted

452
Black wasn't expecting this

453
How to prevent promotion?

454
Worth remembering

455
White's queen is threatened

456
Target a8

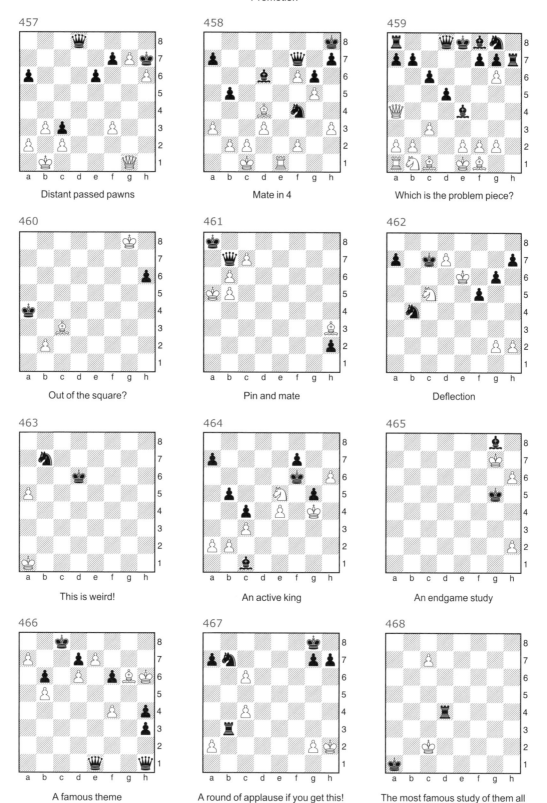

457
Distant passed pawns

458
Mate in 4

459
Which is the problem piece?

460
Out of the square?

461
Pin and mate

462
Deflection

463
This is weird!

464
An active king

465
An endgame study

466
A famous theme

467
A round of applause if you get this!

468
The most famous study of them all

Drawing tactics

White to move
Solutions on page 133

Tactics are not only for winning material or delivering checkmate.

Sometimes the purpose of the most spectacular combinations is to salvage a draw in what at first sight appears to be a lost position. A startling tactical blow that secures a draw by perpetual check or stalemate is just as rewarding as a brilliant checkmate. Few things are as satisfying as 'swindling' our opponent out of what appeared to be certain victory. Remember, the ability to tenaciously defend is as important as the ability to attack!

The most frequent opportunities to give perpetual check are based on sacrifices that smash open the protection of the castled king.

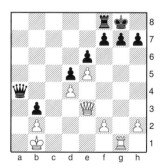

White's position is critical: Black's threat is the devastating 1... ♕a2+.

However, salvation is at hand with:

1. ♖xg7+! ♔xg7 2. ♕g5+ ♔h8 3. ♕f6+ ♔g8 4. ♕g5+ and perpetual check. If Black tries 1... ♔h8, White has 2. ♖xh7+! ♔xh7 3. ♕h3+ ♔g6 4. ♕g4+ ♔h7 3. ♕h5+ etc.

Stalemate and perpetual check are n't the only means for securing the draw. There is also the liquidation sacrifices, where the objective is to simplify to a theoretically drawn endgame position. It should be noted that tactics are as important in the endgame as in the opening and middlegame.

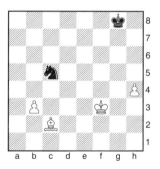

Notwithstanding that White has a two pawn to zero advantage, Black immediately draws by eliminating the only dangerous pawn: 1... ♘xb3! 2. ♗xb3+ ♔h8. Black knows his endgame theory; if the white bishop does not control the queening square, it's a draw.

71

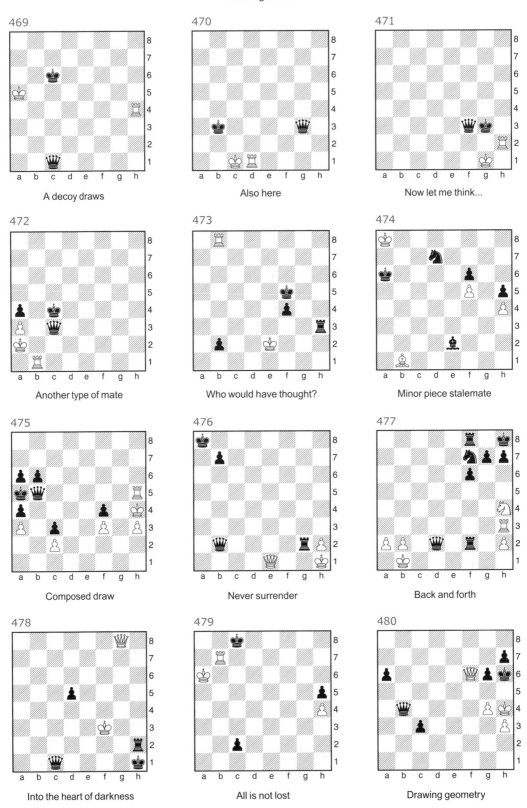

469
A decoy draws

470
Also here

471
Now let me think...

472
Another type of mate

473
Who would have thought?

474
Minor piece stalemate

475
Composed draw

476
Never surrender

477
Back and forth

478
Into the heart of darkness

479
All is not lost

480
Drawing geometry

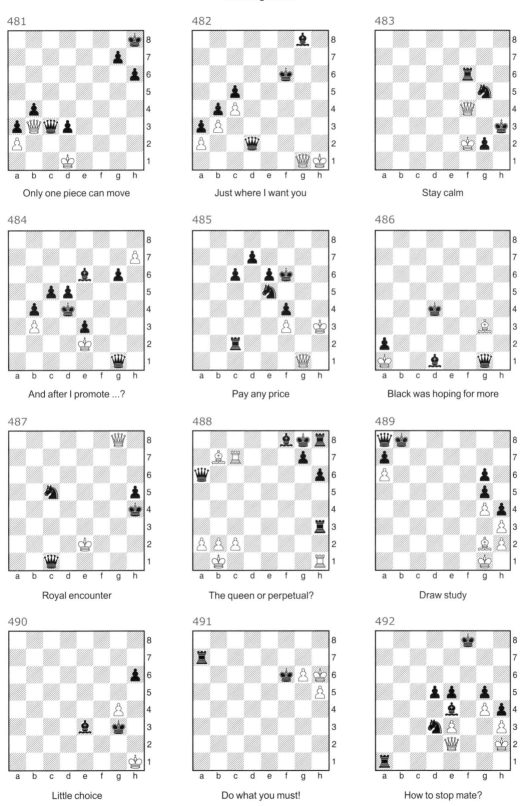

481 Only one piece can move

482 Just where I want you

483 Stay calm

484 And after I promote ...?

485 Pay any price

486 Black was hoping for more

487 Royal encounter

488 The queen or perpetual?

489 Draw study

490 Little choice

491 Do what you must!

492 How to stop mate?

Mixed motifs: White

In the following exercises a variety of motifs are employed. White moves and wins, often using a combination of different tactical elements. Over the board, individual tactical motifs are often hidden in the complexity of the position, and a player must train his eye to recognise how a combination of tactical themes can be put together to achieve his objective, be it mate or winning material.

Solutions on page 133

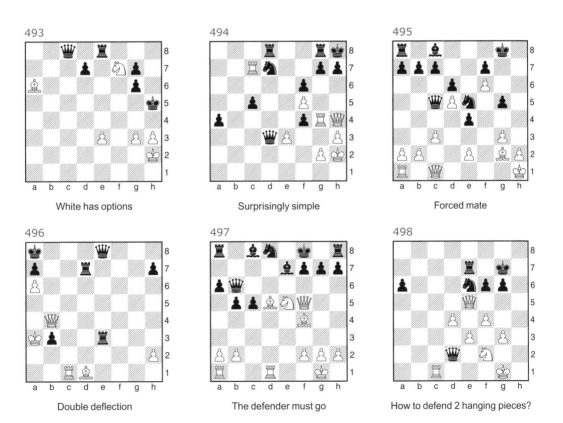

493
White has options

494
Surprisingly simple

495
Forced mate

496
Double deflection

497
The defender must go

498
How to defend 2 hanging pieces?

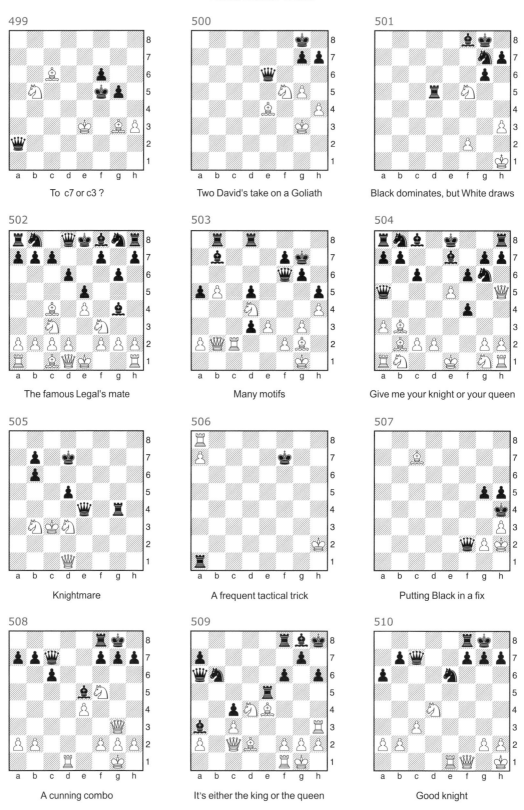

499
To c7 or c3 ?

500
Two David's take on a Goliath

501
Black dominates, but White draws

502
The famous Legal's mate

503
Many motifs

504
Give me your knight or your queen

505
Knightmare

506
A frequent tactical trick

507
Putting Black in a fix

508
A cunning combo

509
It's either the king or the queen

510
Good knight

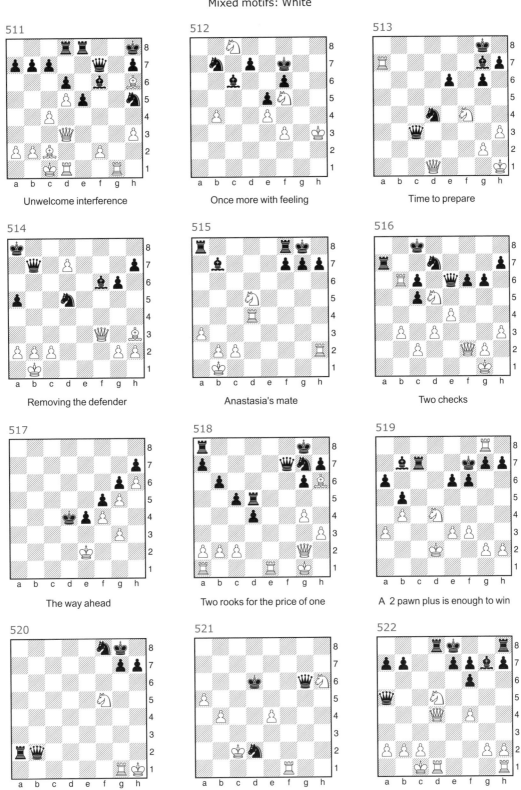

511
Unwelcome interference

512
Once more with feeling

513
Time to prepare

514
Removing the defender

515
Anastasia's mate

516
Two checks

517
The way ahead

518
Two rooks for the price of one

519
A 2 pawn plus is enough to win

520
Again and again and again and...

521
The old one-two

522
Deflection

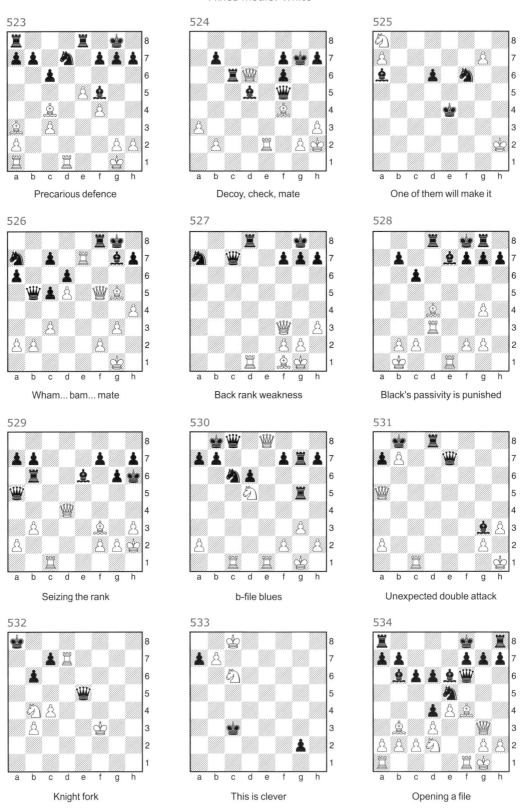

523
Precarious defence

524
Decoy, check, mate

525
One of them will make it

526
Wham... bam... mate

527
Back rank weakness

528
Black's passivity is punished

529
Seizing the rank

530
b-file blues

531
Unexpected double attack

532
Knight fork

533
This is clever

534
Opening a file

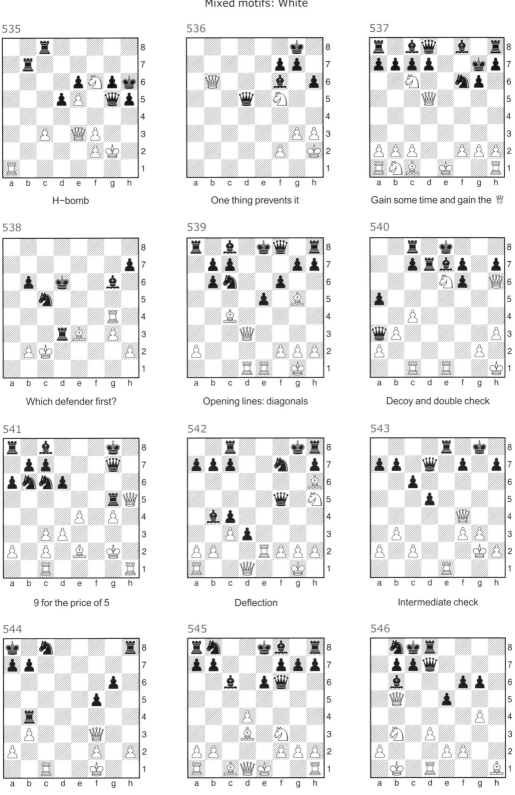

535

H-bomb

536

One thing prevents it

537

Gain some time and gain the ♛

538

Which defender first?

539

Opening lines: diagonals

540

Decoy and double check

541

9 for the price of 5

542

Deflection

543

Intermediate check

544

Double threat

545

Easier than you would think

546

A pin makes it possible

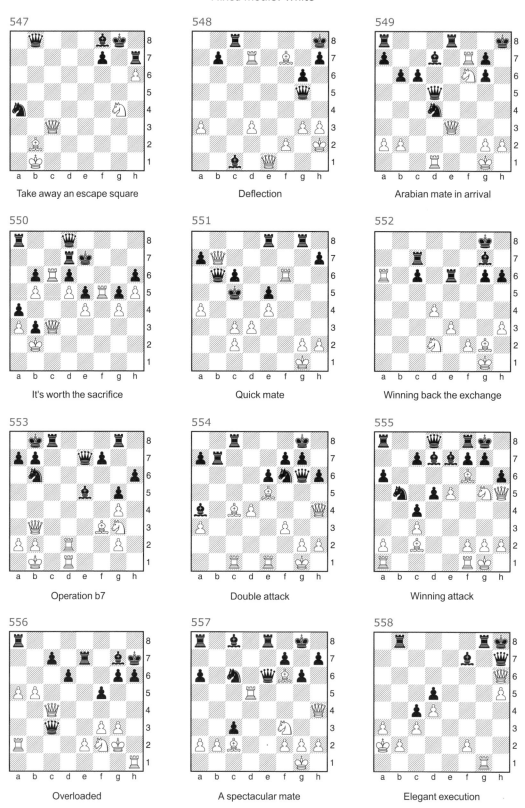

547
Take away an escape square

548
Deflection

549
Arabian mate in arrival

550
It's worth the sacrifice

551
Quick mate

552
Winning back the exchange

553
Operation b7

554
Double attack

555
Winning attack

556
Overloaded

557
A spectacular mate

558
Elegant execution

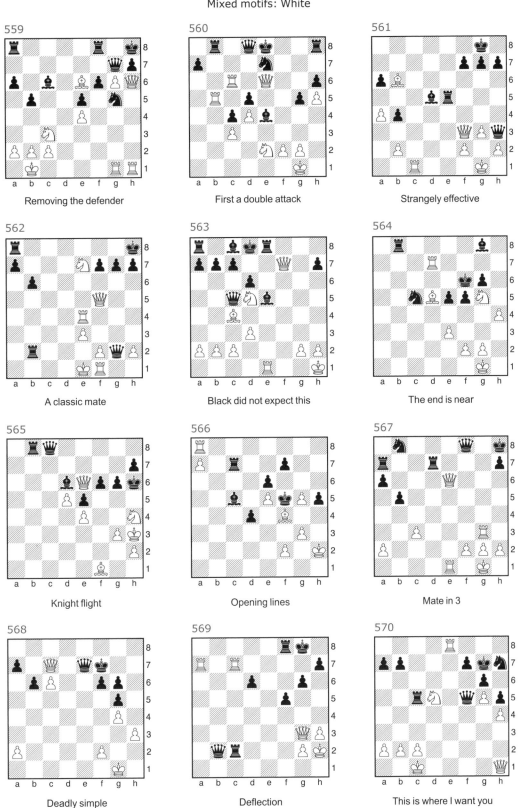

559
Removing the defender

560
First a double attack

561
Strangely effective

562
A classic mate

563
Black did not expect this

564
The end is near

565
Knight flight

566
Opening lines

567
Mate in 3

568
Deadly simple

569
Deflection

570
This is where I want you

81

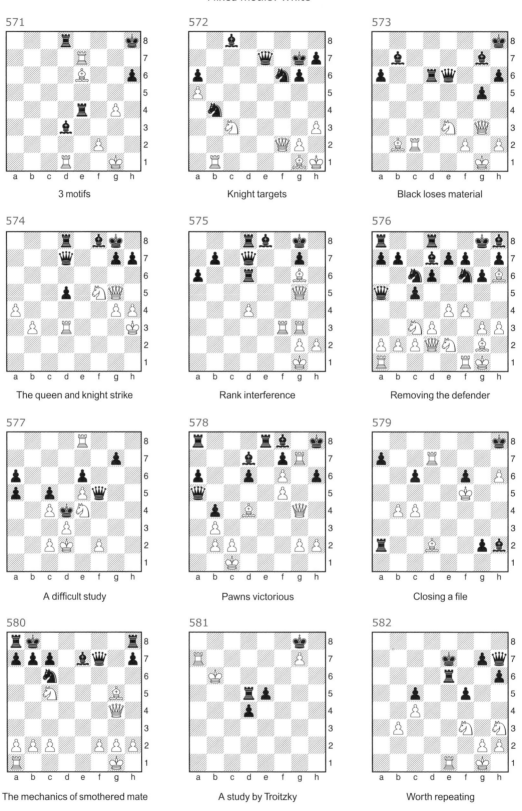

571
3 motifs

572
Knight targets

573
Black loses material

574
The queen and knight strike

575
Rank interference

576
Removing the defender

577
A difficult study

578
Pawns victorious

579
Closing a file

580
The mechanics of smothered mate

581
A study by Troitzky

582
Worth repeating

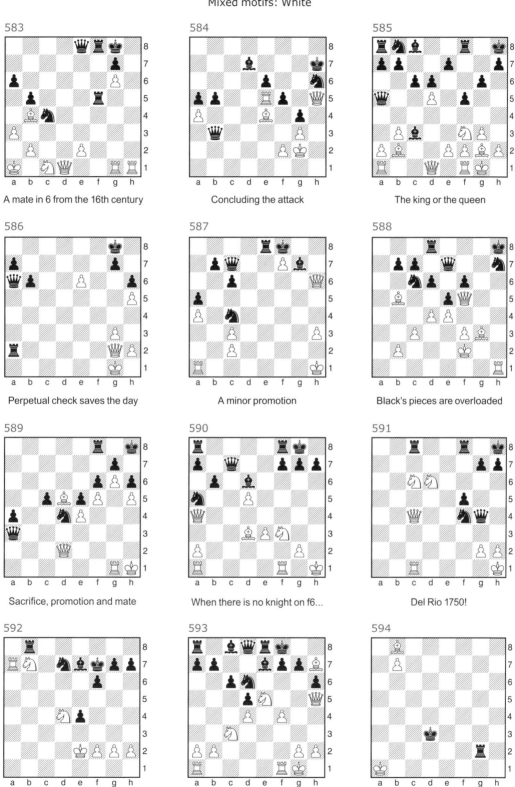

583
A mate in 6 from the 16th century

584
Concluding the attack

585
The king or the queen

586
Perpetual check saves the day

587
A minor promotion

588
Black's pieces are overloaded

589
Sacrifice, promotion and mate

590
When there is no knight on f6...

591
Del Rio 1750!

592
Finishes with a fork

593
Surrounded by friend and foe

594
Crafty bishop

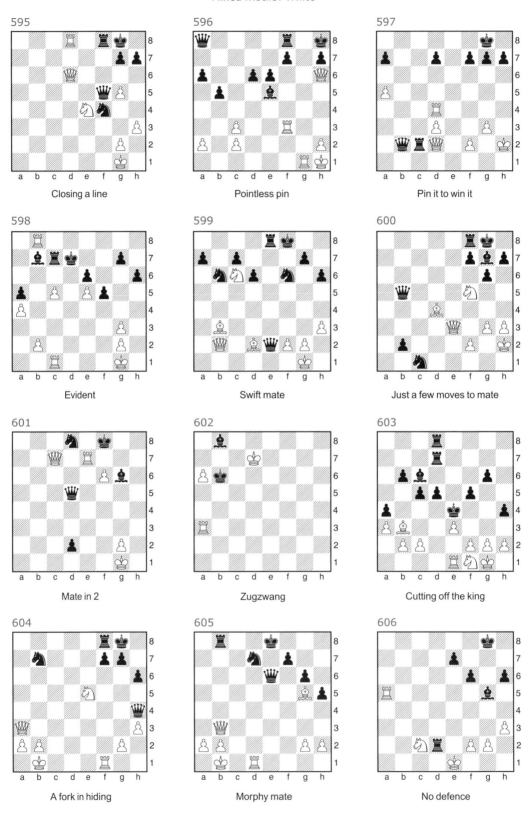

595
Closing a line

596
Pointless pin

597
Pin it to win it

598
Evident

599
Swift mate

600
Just a few moves to mate

601
Mate in 2

602
Zugzwang

603
Cutting off the king

604
A fork in hiding

605
Morphy mate

606
No defence

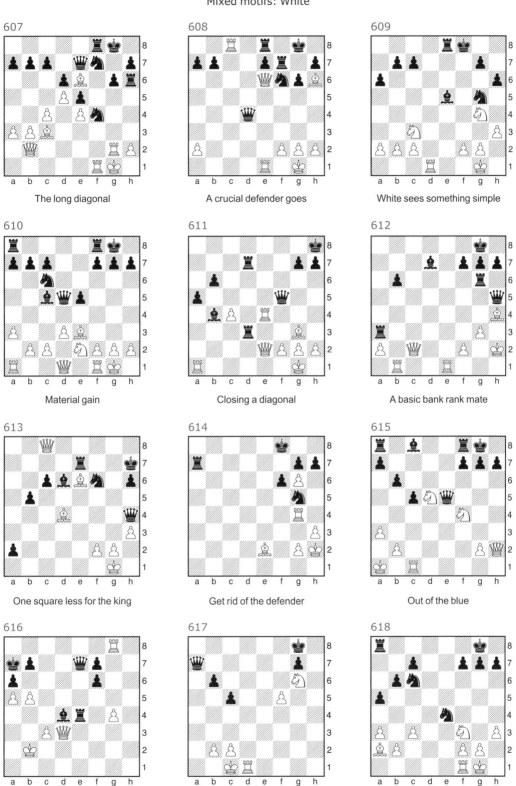

607
The long diagonal

608
A crucial defender goes

609
White sees something simple

610
Material gain

611
Closing a diagonal

612
A basic bank rank mate

613
One square less for the king

614
Get rid of the defender

615
Out of the blue

616
The problem is eliminated

617
Mate is on the way

618
Double on the diagonal

85

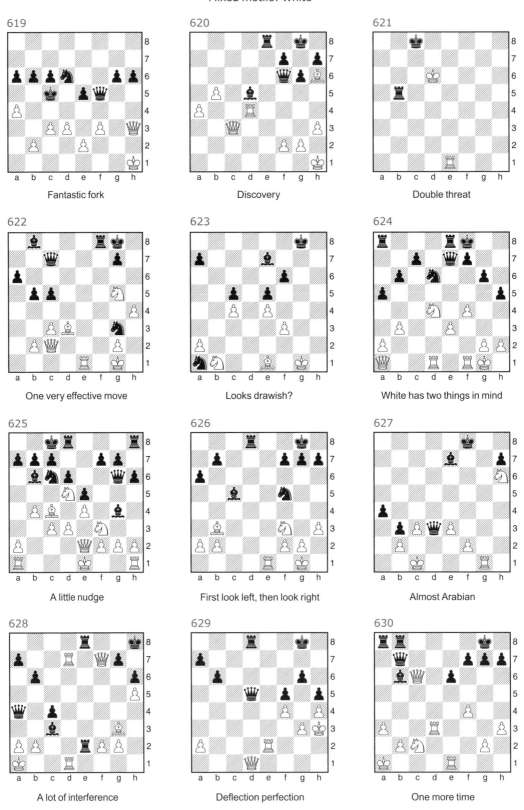

619
Fantastic fork

620
Discovery

621
Double threat

622
One very effective move

623
Looks drawish?

624
White has two things in mind

625
A little nudge

626
First look left, then look right

627
Almost Arabian

628
A lot of interference

629
Deflection perfection

630
One more time

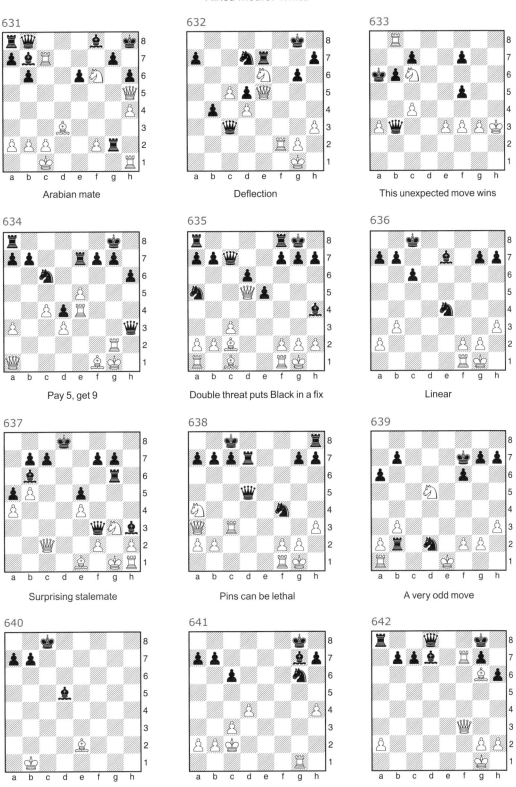

631
Arabian mate

632
Deflection

633
This unexpected move wins

634
Pay 5, get 9

635
Double threat puts Black in a fix

636
Linear

637
Surprising stalemate

638
Pins can be lethal

639
A very odd move

640
Surely White has lost

641
A nasty pawn

642
Vacating a square

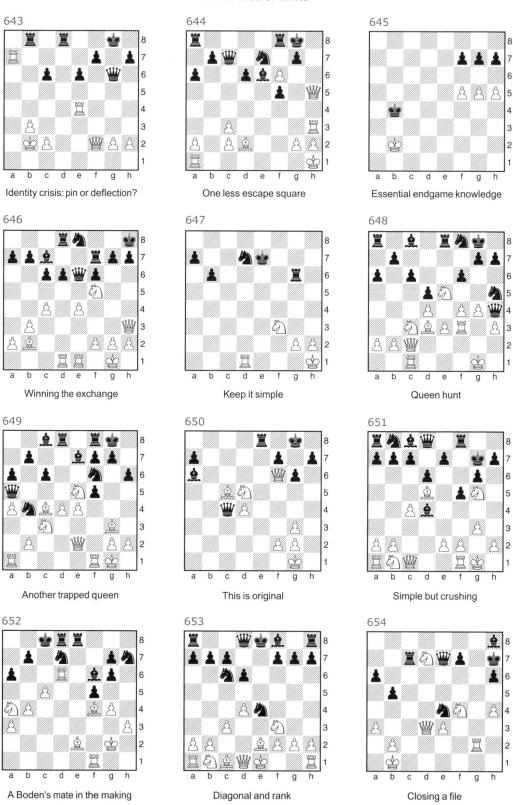

643

Identity crisis: pin or deflection?

644

One less escape square

645

Essential endgame knowledge

646

Winning the exchange

647

Keep it simple

648

Queen hunt

649

Another trapped queen

650

This is original

651

Simple but crushing

652

A Boden's mate in the making

653

Diagonal and rank

654

Closing a file

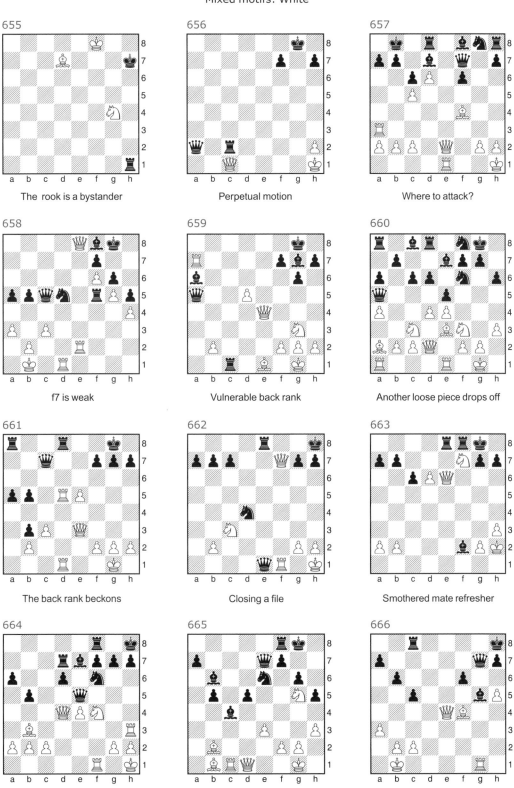

655
The rook is a bystander

656
Perpetual motion

657
Where to attack?

658
f7 is weak

659
Vulnerable back rank

660
Another loose piece drops off

661
The back rank beckons

662
Closing a file

663
Smothered mate refresher

664
Keep your eye on g6

665
Crashing through

666
Opening a diagonal

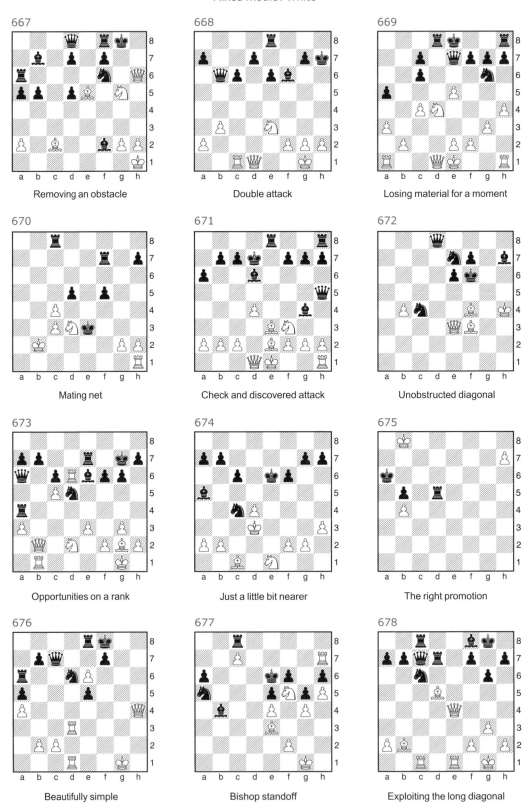

667
Removing an obstacle

668
Double attack

669
Losing material for a moment

670
Mating net

671
Check and discovered attack

672
Unobstructed diagonal

673
Opportunities on a rank

674
Just a little bit nearer

675
The right promotion

676
Beautifully simple

677
Bishop standoff

678
Exploiting the long diagonal

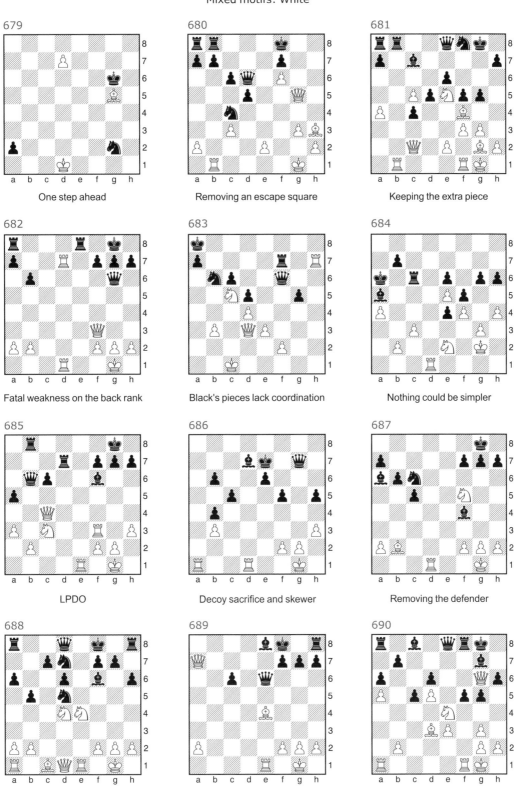

679
One step ahead

680
Removing an escape square

681
Keeping the extra piece

682
Fatal weakness on the back rank

683
Black's pieces lack coordination

684
Nothing could be simpler

685
LPDO

686
Decoy sacrifice and skewer

687
Removing the defender

688
What was that about loose pieces?

689
Discovery

690
Overload

Mixed motifs: Black

As with the previous chapter, a variety of motifs are presented - often with several tactical themes in the one position. However, in these exercises it is Black to move and White to suffer.

Solutions on page 137

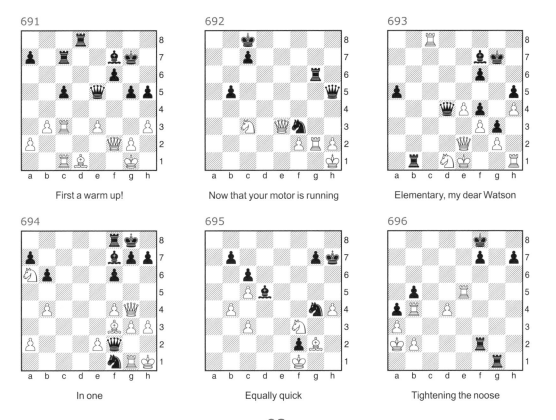

691

First a warm up!

692

Now that your motor is running

693

Elementary, my dear Watson

694

In one

695

Equally quick

696

Tightening the noose

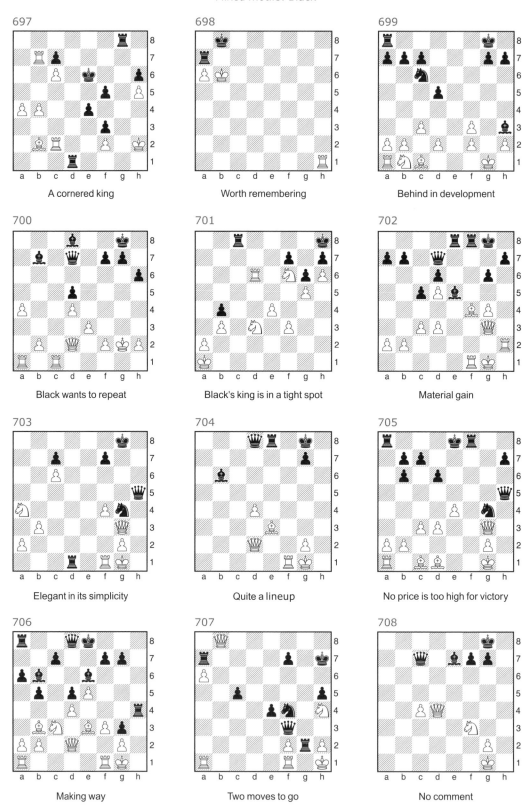

697
A cornered king

698
Worth remembering

699
Behind in development

700
Black wants to repeat

701
Black's king is in a tight spot

702
Material gain

703
Elegant in its simplicity

704
Quite a lineup

705
No price is too high for victory

706
Making way

707
Two moves to go

708
No comment

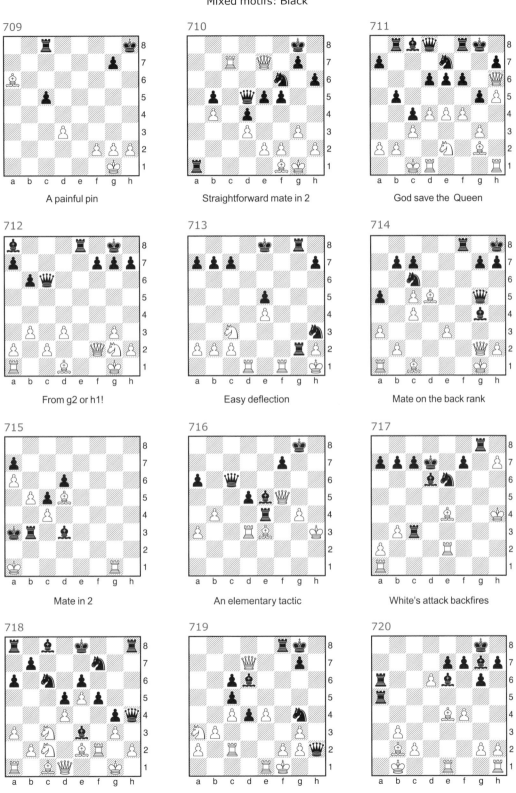

709
A painful pin

710
Straightforward mate in 2

711
God save the Queen

712
From g2 or h1!

713
Easy deflection

714
Mate on the back rank

715
Mate in 2

716
An elementary tactic

717
White's attack backfires

718
Paralysing pin

719
Cutting off the king

720
Deadly two-step

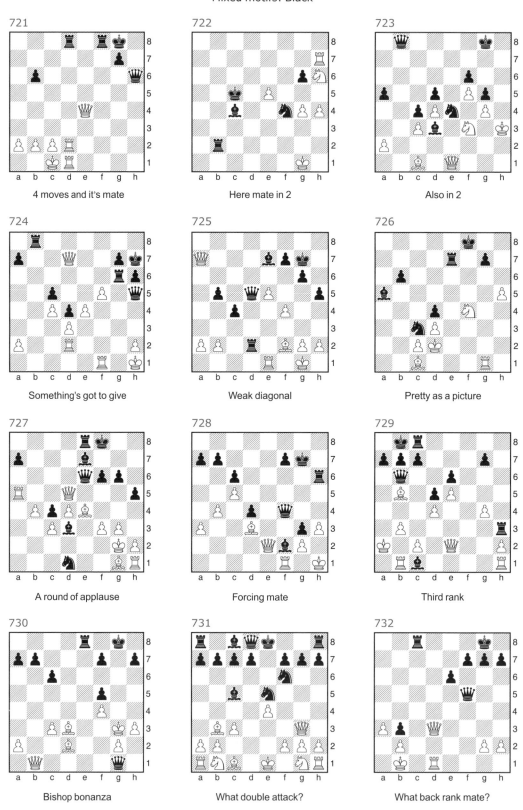

721

4 moves and it's mate

722

Here mate in 2

723

Also in 2

724

Something's got to give

725

Weak diagonal

726

Pretty as a picture

727

A round of applause

728

Forcing mate

729

Third rank

730

Bishop bonanza

731

What double attack?

732

What back rank mate?

96

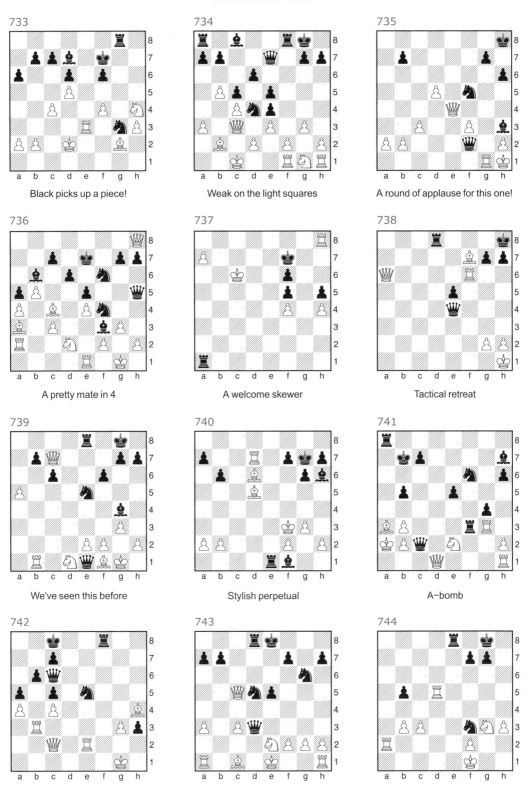

733
Black picks up a piece!

734
Weak on the light squares

735
A round of applause for this one!

736
A pretty mate in 4

737
A welcome skewer

738
Tactical retreat

739
We've seen this before

740
Stylish perpetual

741
A-bomb

742
Made in Italy

743
Double check dynamite

744
I would like to repeat that

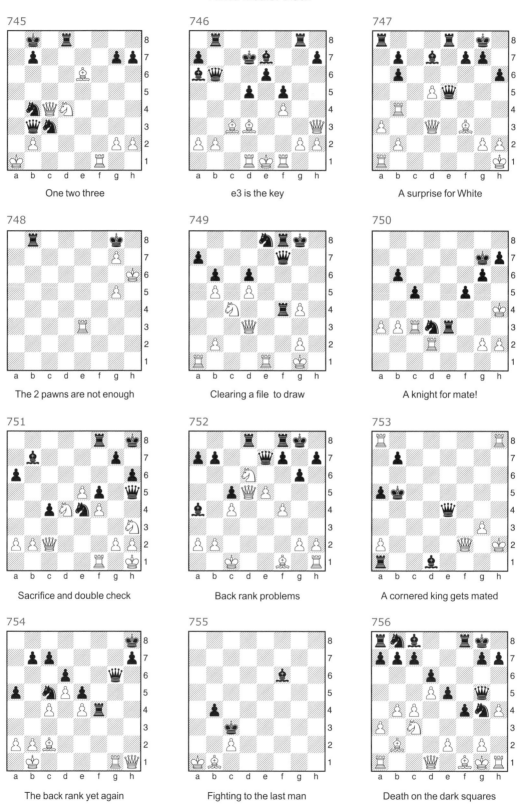

745
One two three

746
e3 is the key

747
A surprise for White

748
The 2 pawns are not enough

749
Clearing a file to draw

750
A knight for mate!

751
Sacrifice and double check

752
Back rank problems

753
A cornered king gets mated

754
The back rank yet again

755
Fighting to the last man

756
Death on the dark squares

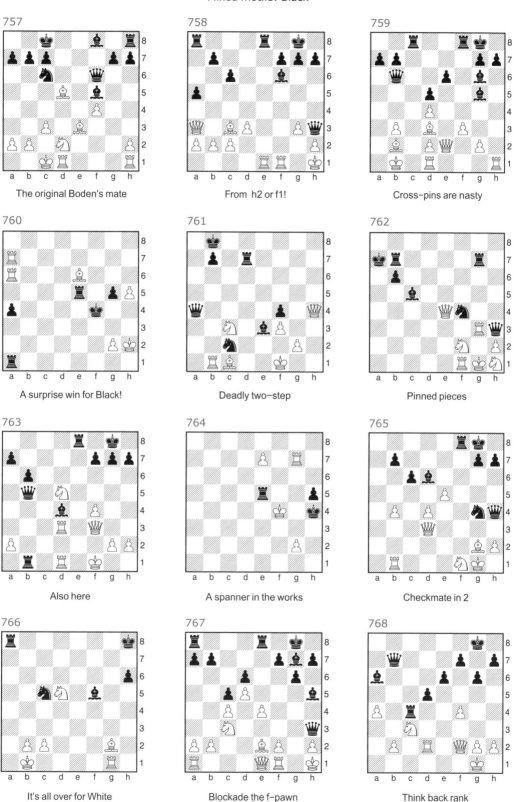

757

The original Boden's mate

758

From h2 or f1!

759

Cross-pins are nasty

760

A surprise win for Black!

761

Deadly two-step

762

Pinned pieces

763

Also here

764

A spanner in the works

765

Checkmate in 2

766

It's all over for White

767

Blockade the f-pawn

768

Think back rank

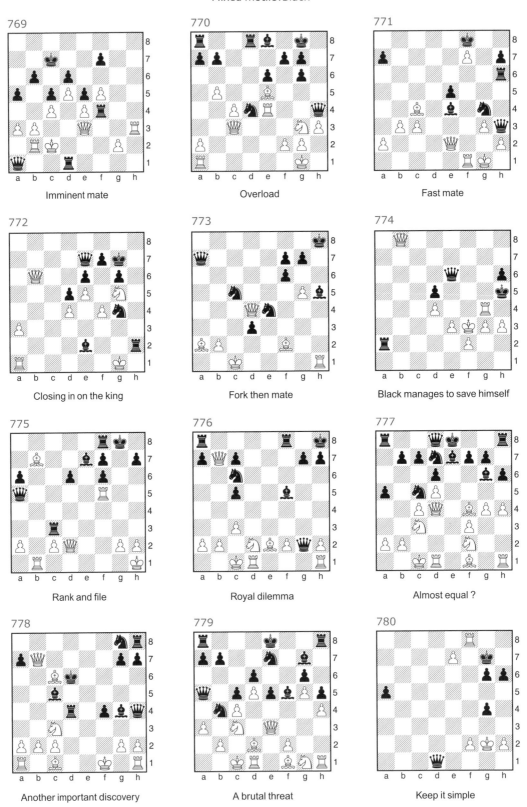

769
Imminent mate

770
Overload

771
Fast mate

772
Closing in on the king

773
Fork then mate

774
Black manages to save himself

775
Rank and file

776
Royal dilemma

777
Almost equal ?

778
Another important discovery

779
A brutal threat

780
Keep it simple

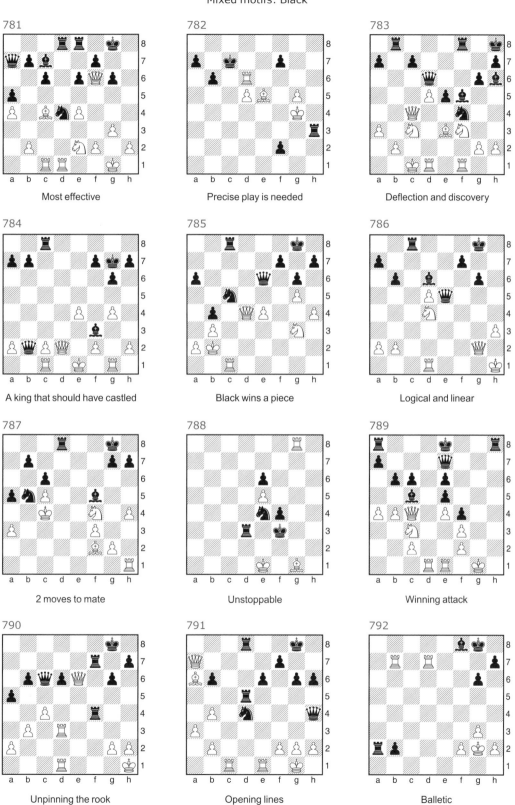

781
Most effective

782
Precise play is needed

783
Deflection and discovery

784
A king that should have castled

785
Black wins a piece

786
Logical and linear

787
2 moves to mate

788
Unstoppable

789
Winning attack

790
Unpinning the rook

791
Opening lines

792
Balletic

101

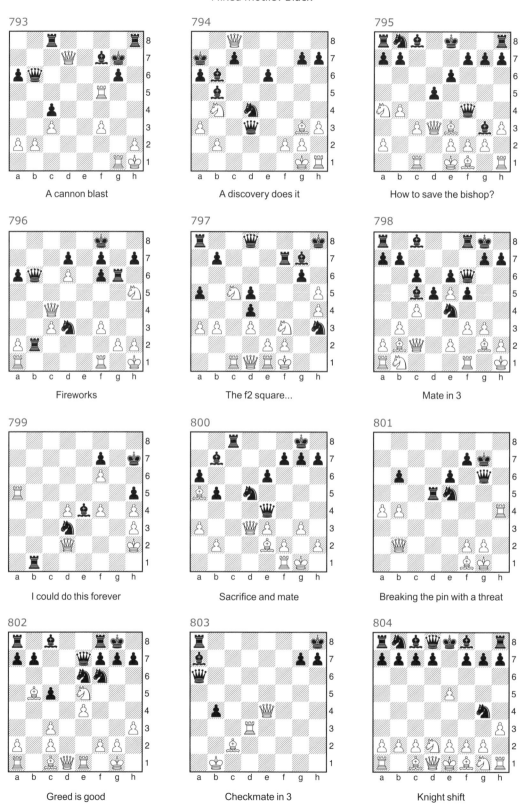

793
A cannon blast

794
A discovery does it

795
How to save the bishop?

796
Fireworks

797
The f2 square...

798
Mate in 3

799
I could do this forever

800
Sacrifice and mate

801
Breaking the pin with a threat

802
Greed is good

803
Checkmate in 3

804
Knight shift

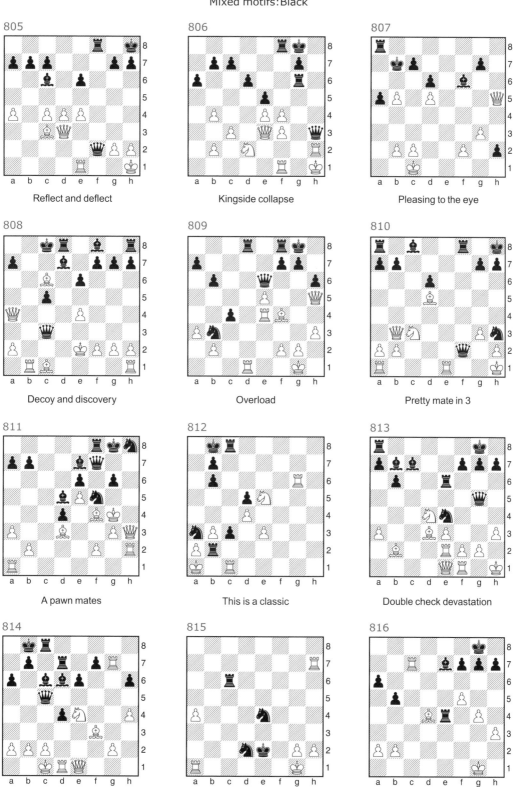

805
Reflect and deflect

806
Kingside collapse

807
Pleasing to the eye

808
Decoy and discovery

809
Overload

810
Pretty mate in 3

811
A pawn mates

812
This is a classic

813
Double check devastation

814
3 more moves to go

815
World Championship tactics

816
Magical rearrangement

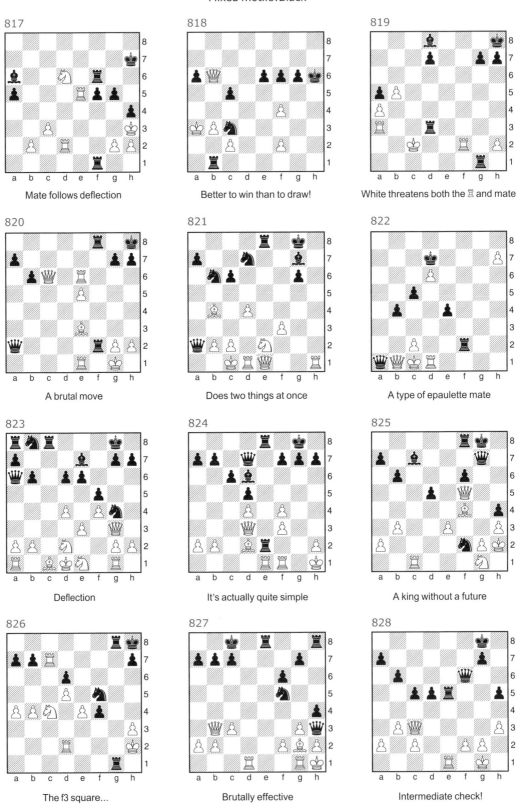

817
Mate follows deflection

818
Better to win than to draw!

819
White threatens both the ♖ and mate

820
A brutal move

821
Does two things at once

822
A type of epaulette mate

823
Deflection

824
It's actually quite simple

825
A king without a future

826
The f3 square...

827
Brutally effective

828
Intermediate check!

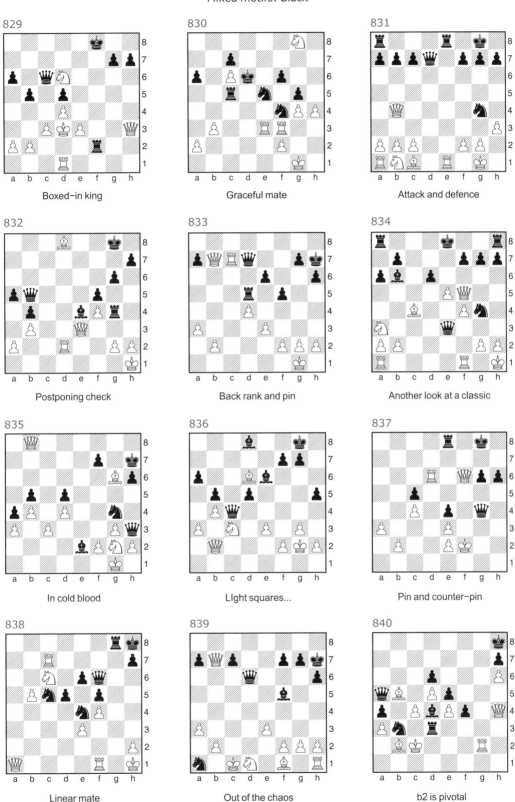

829
Boxed-in king

830
Graceful mate

831
Attack and defence

832
Postponing check

833
Back rank and pin

834
Another look at a classic

835
In cold blood

836
LIght squares...

837
Pin and counter-pin

838
Linear mate

839
Out of the chaos

840
b2 is pivotal

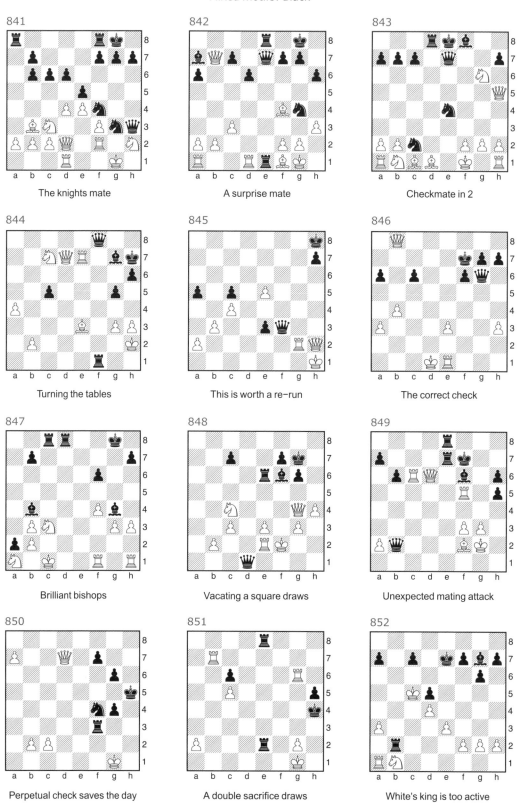

841
The knights mate

842
A surprise mate

843
Checkmate in 2

844
Turning the tables

845
This is worth a re-run

846
The correct check

847
Brilliant bishops

848
Vacating a square draws

849
Unexpected mating attack

850
Perpetual check saves the day

851
A double sacrifice draws

852
White's king is too active

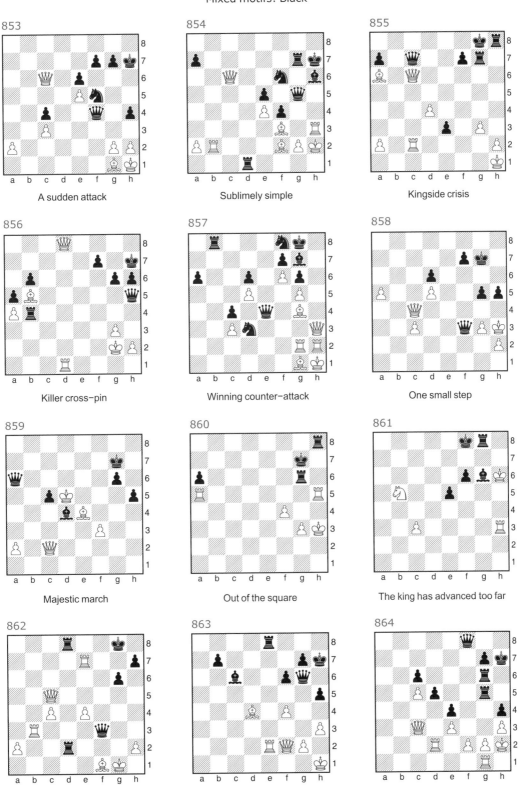

853
A sudden attack

854
Sublimely simple

855
Kingside crisis

856
Killer cross-pin

857
Winning counter-attack

858
One small step

859
Majestic march

860
Out of the square

861
The king has advanced too far

862
Mixed motifs mate

863
It's easy when you know how

864
Firepower on the kingside

Mate in three

White to move and mate in three. The exercises progress from the comparatively easy to the delightfully difficult. Tactical puzzles to test your strength!

Solutions on page 140

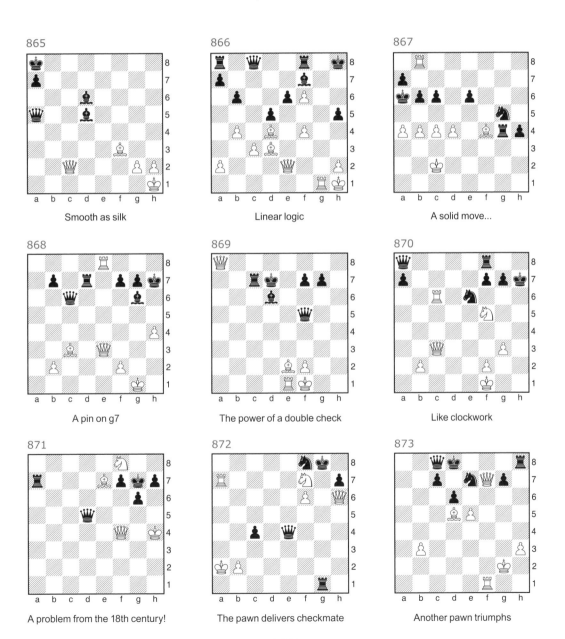

865
Smooth as silk

866
Linear logic

867
A solid move...

868
A pin on g7

869
The power of a double check

870
Like clockwork

871
A problem from the 18th century!

872
The pawn delivers checkmate

873
Another pawn triumphs

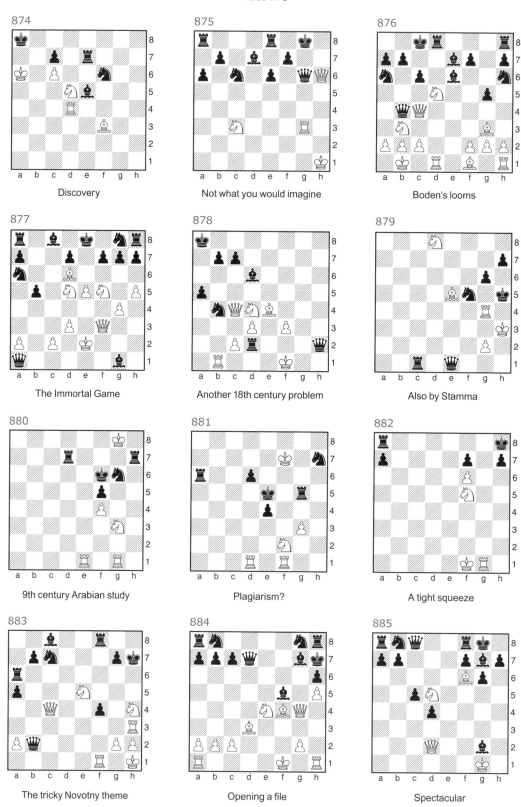

874
Discovery

875
Not what you would imagine

876
Boden's looms

877
The Immortal Game

878
Another 18th century problem

879
Also by Stamma

880
9th century Arabian study

881
Plagiarism?

882
A tight squeeze

883
The tricky Novotny theme

884
Opening a file

885
Spectacular

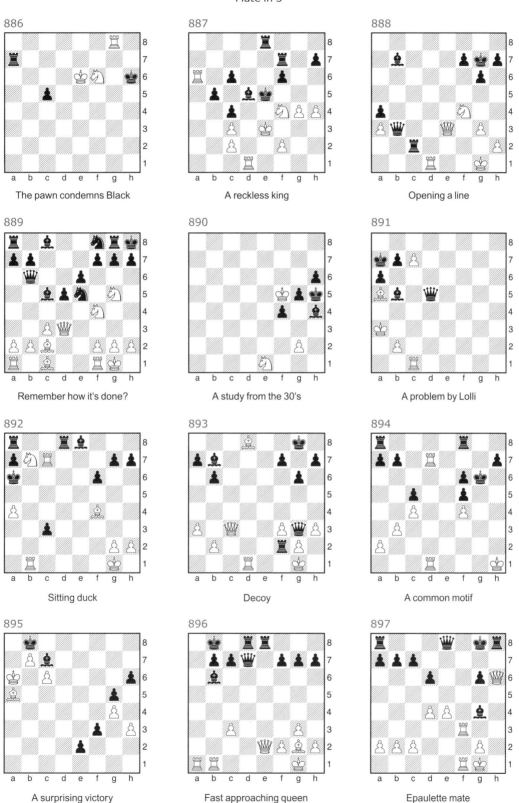

886
The pawn condemns Black

887
A reckless king

888
Opening a line

889
Remember how it's done?

890
A study from the 30's

891
A problem by Lolli

892
Sitting duck

893
Decoy

894
A common motif

895
A surprising victory

896
Fast approaching queen

897
Epaulette mate

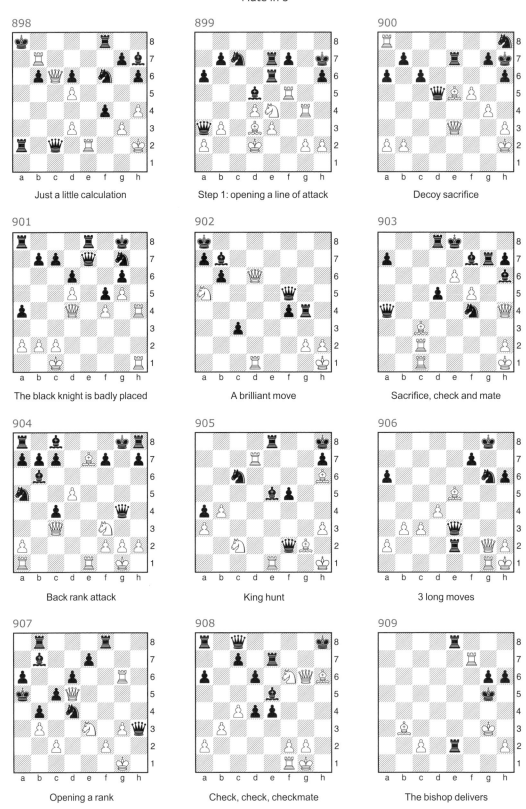

898

Just a little calculation

899

Step 1: opening a line of attack

900

Decoy sacrifice

901

The black knight is badly placed

902

A brilliant move

903

Sacrifice, check and mate

904

Back rank attack

905

King hunt

906

3 long moves

907

Opening a rank

908

Check, check, checkmate

909

The bishop delivers

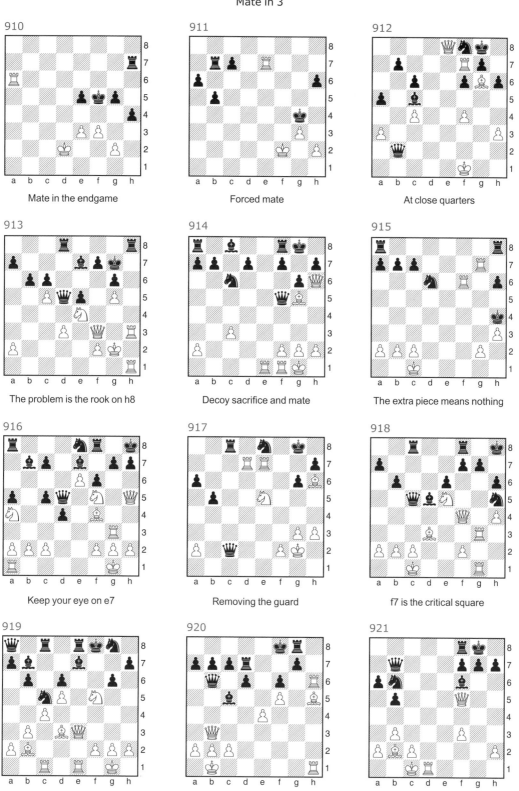

910
Mate in the endgame

911
Forced mate

912
At close quarters

913
The problem is the rook on h8

914
Decoy sacrifice and mate

915
The extra piece means nothing

916
Keep your eye on e7

917
Removing the guard

918
f7 is the critical square

919
Check, sacrifice and mate

920
The h-file

921
Now the g-file

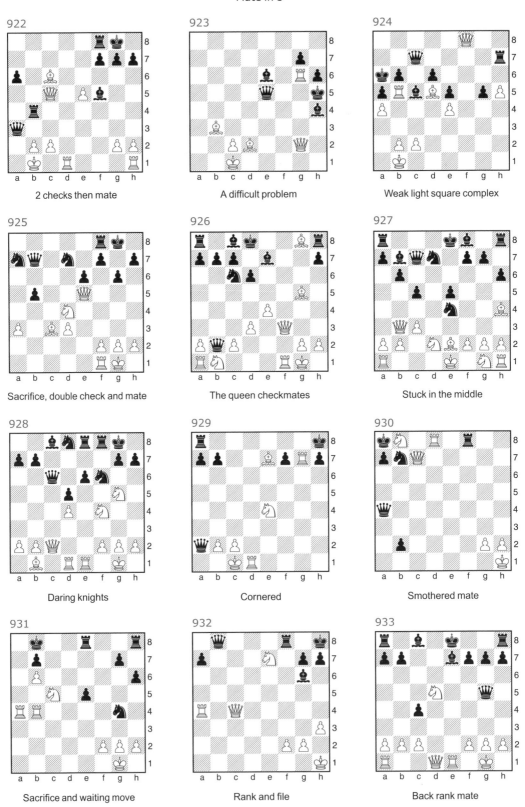

922
2 checks then mate

923
A difficult problem

924
Weak light square complex

925
Sacrifice, double check and mate

926
The queen checkmates

927
Stuck in the middle

928
Daring knights

929
Cornered

930
Smothered mate

931
Sacrifice and waiting move

932
Rank and file

933
Back rank mate

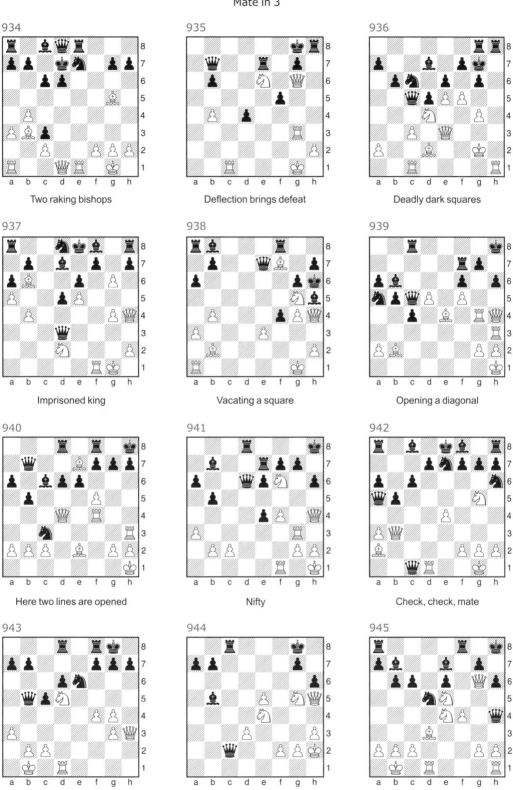

934
Two raking bishops

935
Deflection brings defeat

936
Deadly dark squares

937
Imprisoned king

938
Vacating a square

939
Opening a diagonal

940
Here two lines are opened

941
Nifty

942
Check, check, mate

943
h–file

944
Knight attack

945
Discoveries are dangerous

115

Mate in four

White to move and mate in four moves. Here too the exercises become progressively more difficult; if you finish these, you deserve a diploma!

Solutions on page 142

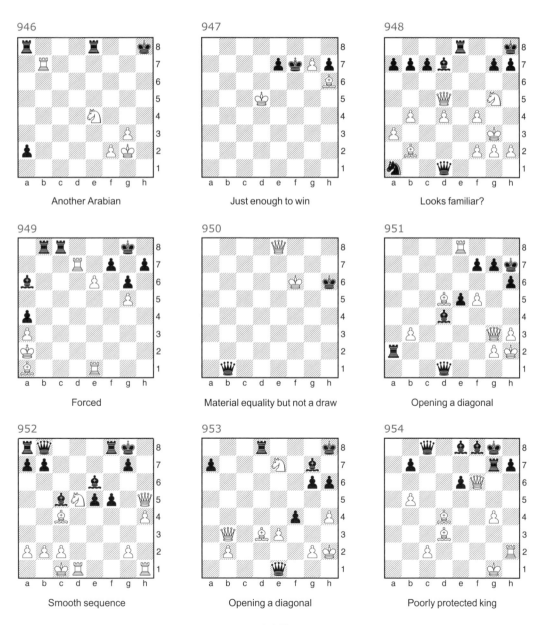

946
Another Arabian

947
Just enough to win

948
Looks familiar?

949
Forced

950
Material equality but not a draw

951
Opening a diagonal

952
Smooth sequence

953
Opening a diagonal

954
Poorly protected king

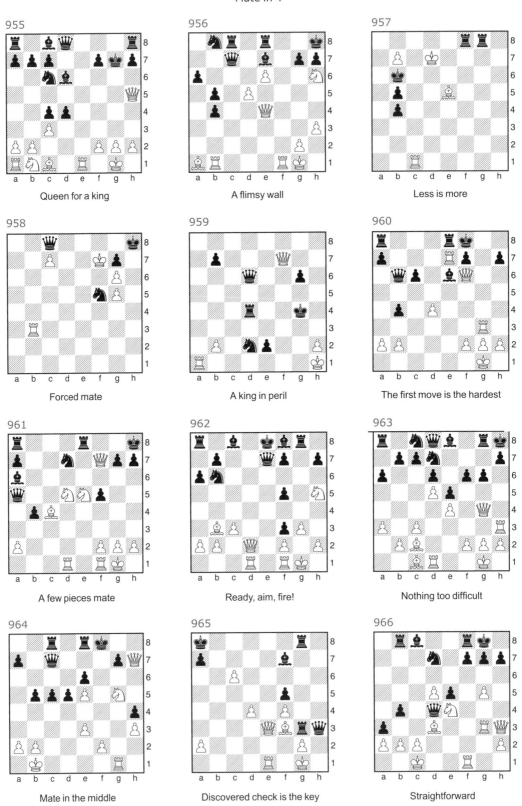

955
Queen for a king

956
A flimsy wall

957
Less is more

958
Forced mate

959
A king in peril

960
The first move is the hardest

961
A few pieces mate

962
Ready, aim, fire!

963
Nothing too difficult

964
Mate in the middle

965
Discovered check is the key

966
Straightforward

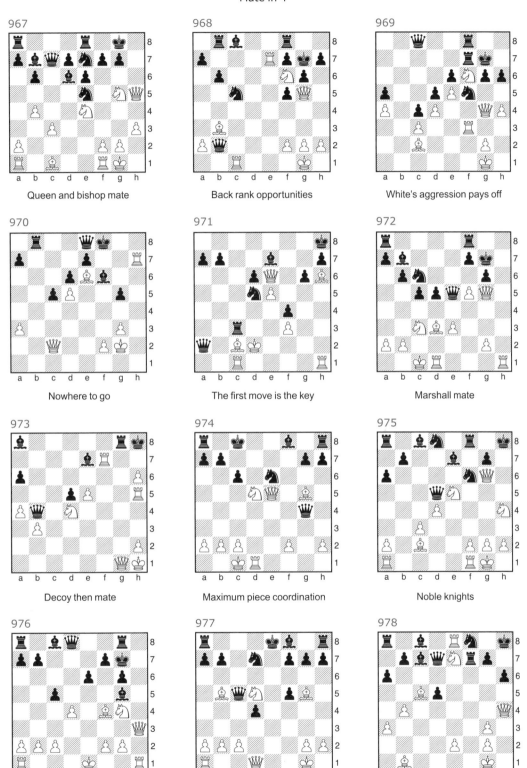

967
Queen and bishop mate

968
Back rank opportunities

969
White's aggression pays off

970
Nowhere to go

971
The first move is the key

972
Marshall mate

973
Decoy then mate

974
Maximum piece coordination

975
Noble knights

976
The path to victory

977
Not so hard really

978
2 bishops are sufficient

Curiosities

Unless indicated, White to move
Solutions on page 142

We conclude with a variety of positions that range from tragicomic resignation with a won position to tactics so exquisite they approach art. Not all our readers will be able to solve these, but this does not prevent us from delighting in the whimsical beauty of tactical opportunities both missed or brilliantly found.

The fact that so many of these positions are from actual games proves that fact is stranger than fiction. However, as elsewhere in the book, some of the following positions are the fruit of a composer's imagination.

Such positions are called 'studies' or 'problems', and though composed, they can be of great value in developing our tactical skills. The first type involves realistic looking positions where the challenge is to find a move sequence that leads to victory, a winning material advantage or a theoretical draw.

In the second type the objective is to find mate in a certain number of moves; in these problems it is of no importance if White has such a decisive advantage that he could win with inaccurate play; the solver must indicate the only solution that leads to checkmate in two, three or more moves.

To whet your appetite here is a celebrated problem created by Sam Loyd in 1859.

White to move and mate in two. The solution is 1. ♕a5!!; each reply by Black results in a different way to checkmate: if 1... ♗c5 2. ♕a1#, if 1... ♗e7 2. ♕e5#, if 1... ♖d7 2. ♘f5#, if 1... ♖e7 2. ♕xb4# and so on. You may enjoy finding the remaining ways to deliver mate!

We will finish with a word of warning: being a good tactician does not mean that we have to make startling sacrifices and tactical skirmishes at all costs. Tactics are not an end in themselves, but rather a tool that must bring concrete advantages or make it possible to execute our plans. The use of tactics requires not only creativity and courage, but also prudent

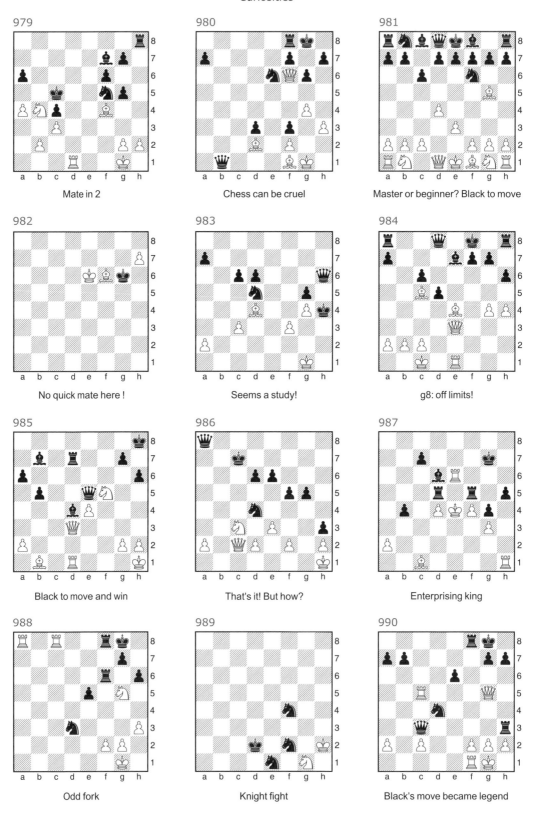

979
Mate in 2

980
Chess can be cruel

981
Master or beginner? Black to move

982
No quick mate here !

983
Seems a study!

984
g8: off limits!

985
Black to move and win

986
That's it! But how?

987
Enterprising king

988
Odd fork

989
Knight fight

990
Black's move became legend

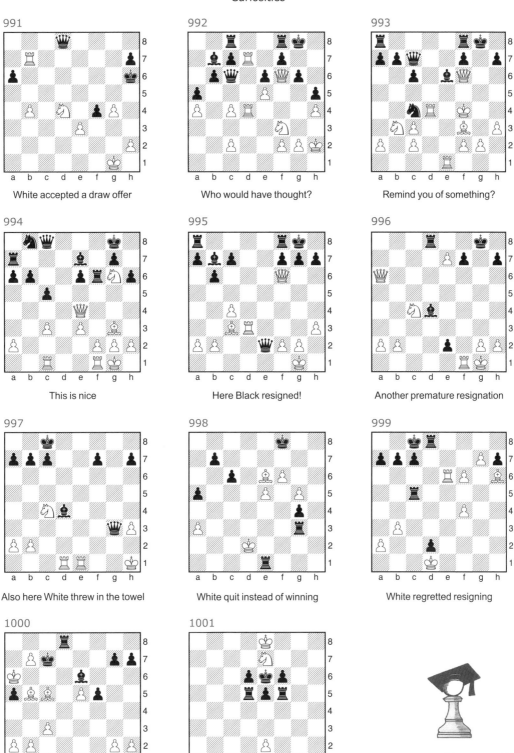

991
White accepted a draw offer

992
Who would have thought?

993
Remind you of something?

994
This is nice

995
Here Black resigned!

996
Another premature resignation

997
Also here White threw in the towel

998
White quit instead of winning

999
White regretted resigning

1000
A clever king !

1001
Megafork

the end!

123

Solutions

Mate in one: page 7

1 – 1.♖xa6#
2 – 1.♗f6#
3 – 1.♖f7#
4 – 1.♖h1#
5 – 1.♖a8#
6 – 1.♘b5#
7 – 1.♗h5#
8 – 1.e4#
9 – 1.f7#
10 – 1.♗f6 #
11 – 1.c8♘#
12 – 1.♕xa7#
13 – 1.g4#
14 – 1.♗xf7#
15 – 1.♘a6#
16 – 1.♗xd6#
17 – 1.♕e7# Anderssen–Staunton 1851
18 – 1.♕e8# Staunton–Anderssen 1851
19 – 1.♕f3# Kovacic–Tasic 2006
20 – 1.♖xh6# 1.♕h7# 1.♘f7#
21 – 1.♖d8#
22 – 1.♖e8# Anderssen–Mayet 1855
23 – 1.g4# 1.♕e4#
24 – 1.♘f6# Staunton–Brodie 1851
25 – 1.♘d6#
26 – 1.♕d6#
27 – 1.♕b5# Zukertort–Anderssen 1865
28 – 1.♕a8#
29 – 1.♘c4#
30 – 1.♕d8# Adams–Leko 2005
31 – 1.♕f7# Lange–Anderssen 1859
32 – 1.♕e5# Greco–NN 1620
33 – 1.♕xh5# Petrosian–Kortchnoi 1977
34 – 1.♕f6# Nadig–Vinas 2006
35 – 1.♗e8#
36 – 1.♕d6# Nepomniachtchi–Sharma 2006
37 – 1.♗g6#

38 – 1.♖g8# Kortchnoi–Padevsky 1972
39 – 1.♘f7#
40 – 1.♘xf6#
41 – 1.♘c6# 1.♘ed7#
42 – 1.♖g5#
43 – 1.♗xd7#
44 – 1.♗g5#
45 – 1.gxh8♘#
46 – 1.♖e8#
47 – 1.♘f7#
48 – 1.♖h5#
49 – 1.♘d3#
50 – 1.♕a8# Shaw–Tcharotchkin 2006
51 – 1.♘d8# Bets–Melnikov 2005
52 – 1.♕h4# Marshall–Mason 1902
53 – 1.♘f5# Gurevich–Markowski 2005
54 – 1.♘xg7#
55 – 1.♖f8# Anderssen–Mieses 1867
56 – 1.♖xf3# Wells–Gonzalez 1995
57 – 1.♕xh7# Bakker–Ocana 2006

Mate in two: page 13

58 – 1.♗g5+ ♔e8 2.♖h8#
59 – 1.♖h8+! (decoy sacrifice) 1... ♔xh8 2.♕h7#
60 – 1.♕xg4+! ♔xg4 2.♗e2#
61 – 1.♕xh6+ ♔xh6 2.♖h8#
62 – 1.♕xf6+! ♔xf6 2.♗d4#
63 – 1.♕g8+! ♖xg8 2.♘f7#
64 – 1.♖h5+! gxh5 2.♕f6#
65 – 1.♘xf5+! gxf5 2.fxg5#
66 – 1.♕xg6+! hxg6 2.♖h8#
67 – 1.♖xe5+! ♘xe5 2.♖d8#
68 – 1.♖e8+!! ♔xe8 2.♖g8#
69 – 1.♖f8+! (decoy sacrifice) 1...♔xf8 2.♕f7#
70 – 1.♘f6 ♕xf6 [1...♖g8 2.♕xh7#] 2.♕xf8#
71 – 1.♕e8+! ♘xe8 2.♖f8#
72 – 1.♖cg7 g2 2.♖g8# the same mate follows other moves

125

73 – 1.♖e8+ double check 1...♔g7 2.h6#

74 – 1.♖e8+ ♕xe8 deflection [1...♗xe8 inter-ference 2.♕g8#] 2.♕xf6#

75 – 1.♕e1+! ♖xe1 2.g3#

76 – 1.♕xf6! gxf6 2.♗xf6#

77 – 1.♖h3+ ♔g8 2.♖h8#

78 – 1.♕xf6+! ♘g7 [1...♘xf6 2.♗xf6#] 2.♕xg7#

79 – 1.♖xh7+! ♔xh7 2.♕h5#

80–1.♕xf8+ [1.♖g4+ ♖xg4 (1...♔xg4 2.♕xf8#) 2.♕xf8#] 1...♔xf8 2.♖g4#

81 – 1.♖a6!! bxa6 2.b7# a problem by Morphy

82 – 1.♕d6+ a pin 1...♕d7 only move 2.♕xd7#

83 – 1.♘c3! ♘b1 [1...♘c4 2.♘f3#] 2.♘f3#

84 – 1.♕f7+!! ♗xf7 2.♘e6#

85 – 1.♕g7+!! ♘xg7 2.♘h6#

86 – 1.♗a6! e1♕ 2.♗b5#

87 – 1.♕e7+ ♘xe7 2.♘f6#

88 – 1.♘f6 ♘c6 a ♖ move does not stop mate either 2.♖h7#

89 – 1.♘g6+! hxg6 2.♖h1#

90 – 1.♕xc6+!! bxc6 2.♖b8#

91 – 1.♕xc6+!! bxc6 2.♗a6#

92 – 1.♕c6+!! bxc6 2.♗a6#

93 – 1.♘c6! f3 no other move by Black can prevent 2.♖a8#

94 – 1.♗f8 c1♕ no alternative move by Black can stop 2.♕g7#

95 – 1.a8♘+! ♔a5 2.♖a7#

96 – 1.♘e7+ ♔h8 2.♗f6#

97 – 1.♖xf7!! ♖xf7 2.♖g8#

98 – 1.♕g6+! hxg6 [1...♖f7 2.♕xf7#] 2.♘g7#

99 –1.♕e6+! ♗xe6 [1...♘xe6 2.♘h6#] 2.♘h6#

100 - 1.♕xd7+! ♘xd7 2.♖e8#

101– 1.♕b6 ♕xe5 it is impossible to stop 2.♕xb7#

102 – 1.♕xa7+!! (eliminating the defender of the b5 square) 1...♖xa7 2.b5#

103 – 1.♖1d6+! ♗c6 2.♖b7#

104 – 1.♔f5! zugzwang 1...g4 forced 2.hxg4#

105 – 1.♗c5! f1♕ it is impossible to stop 2.a7#

106 –1.♗e7+ discovered check 1...♔h8 2.♗f6#

107 – 1.♗a7!! threatening ♗c5# 1...c6 [1...c5 2.♗b8#] 2.♗b8#

108 –1.♖f8+! ♕xf8 2.♕xh7#

109 – 1.♕e8+! ♕xe8 2.♘xf6#

110 – 1.♕xe5+! ♖xe5 [1...♔g8 2.♕g7#] 2.♖xd8#

111 – 1.♘g6+! fxg6 2.♕e8#

112 – 1.♕h5+! gxh5 2.♘f5#

113 – 1.♕xh5+! gxh5 2.♖h6#

114 – 1.♕xe8+! ♔xe8 2.♖d8#

115 – 1.♕e4+! ♔xe4 2.♘f6#

116 – 1.♕xb8+ ♕xb8 2.♘b6#

117 – 1.♖xg7+! ♔xf6 [1...♔e8 2.♖e7#] 2.♕d4#

118 – 1.♔f7+ discovered check 1...♕xa8 2.g7#

119 – 1.♖e7! ♕xf7 2.♖xf7#

120 – 1.♕xe6+! fxe6 2.♗g6#

121 – 1.♖d7+! ♔xd7 2.♘f7#

122 – 1.♖h8+! ♔xh8 2.f7#

123 – 1.♕g8+! ♔xg8 2.♗e6#

124 – 1.♖e8+! ♖xe8 [1...♕xe8 2.♕xg7#] 2.♕xg7#

125 – 1.♕xh6+! gxh6 2.♘f7#

126 – 1.♕xf6+! decoy sacrifice 1...♔xf6 2.♗d4#

127 – 1.♕g7+!! ♔xg7 2.♖xg6#

128 – 1.♘b4 g1♕ and 2.♘xa6# can't be stopped

129 –1.♖h4 d4 Black can't stop 2.♖h8#

130 – 1.♖d7 g5 Black can't prevent 2.♖xa7#

131 – 1.d6! f1♕ and 2.♖e7# can't be stopped

132 –1.g5+ ♔xg5 forced 2.♕f4#

133 – 1.♕a3+ ♔xa3 2.♘c2#

134 – 1.♖d4+ exd4 2.♖f4#

135 – 1.♕f8+! ♖xf8 2.♖xf8#

136 – 1.d4!! the Novotny theme: either cap-ture on d4 will obstruct the action of the other black piece. 1...hxg6 [1...♖xd4 2.♘e5#; 1...♗xd4 2.♘d2#] 2.♘d2# (study by Troitzky)

137 – 1.♘g6+ ♔g8 2.♗e6#

138 – 1.♕xf8+ ♕xf8 2.♖xh7#

139 – 1.♖d8+! ♖xd8 2.♕xe6#

140 – 1.♕xg7+!! ♘xg7 2.♘h6#

141 – 1.♕h6+ ♔g8 2.♕g7#

142 – 1.♔c2 g3 Black can not prevent 2.♖f4#

143 – 1.e8♕+ ♖xe8 [1...♕xe8 2.♕d6#] 2.♕c7#

144 – 1.♖h6+ ♗xh6 [1...♔xh6 2.♕h2#] 2.♕g8# Ramaswany–Delai 1988

145 – 1.♖h4+ ♘xh4 2.♗g7#

146 – 1.♘b3+ axb3 2.♖a1#

147 – 1.♖xh5+ gxh5 2.g6#

148 – 1.♖f6+ ♗xf6 2.♕xf6#

149 – 1.♕h8+ ♔xh8 2.♖xf8#

150 – 1.♖xf6+ ♘xf6 2.♕f7#

151 – 1.♖e4+ ♔xd5 2.♘f6#

152 – 1.♕h8+ ♔xh8 2.♖f7#

153 – 1.♖e4+ ♔xe4 2.♖e6#

154 – 1.♕xh6+ ♔xh6 2.♘f5#

155 – 1.♖e6+ ♔xe6 2.♕d6#

156 – 1.♕d6+ ♖xd6 2.♖f7#
157 – 1.♖f5+ ♖xf5 2.♘e6#
158 – 1.♖f5+ ♔xf5 2.d4#
159 – 1.♗g7+ ♔xg7 2.♕h7#
160 – 1.♖f5+ ♗xf5 2.♘f4#
161 – 1.♗f8+ gxh5 2.♖h6#
162 – 1.♖f5+ ♔xf5 2.♗h3#
163 – 1.♕xf8+ ♔xf8 2.♖d8#
164 – 1.♕h4+ gxh4 2.♖xh4#
165 – 1.♗xg6+ ♖xg6 2.♕h8#
166 – 1.♕xc6+ ♗xc6 2.♘xe6#
167 – 1.b8♕+ ♘xb8 2.♖d8#
168 – 1.♕d5+ ♔b6 2.♕b5#
169 – 1.♗h6+ ♔g8 2.♖e8#
170 – 1.♖a3+ bxa3 2.b3#
171 – 1.♖e5+ ♔xe5 [1...d6 2.♕b8#] 2.♕e7#
172 – 1.♕g5+ hxg5 [1...♔h3 2.♕xg4#] 2.♕h7#
173 – 1.♘e7+ ♔f8 [1...♔h8 2.♘g6#] 2.♘g6#
174 – 1.e4+ ♔xe4 [1...♔c4 2.♗a6#] 2.♗b7#
175 – 1.♖c8+ ♕xc8 2.♕xd6#
176 – 1.♖xa7+ ♔xa7 2.♕xb6#
177 – 1.♕g7+ ♔xg7 2.h8♕#
178 – 1.♖h8+ ♗xh8 2.♖h7#
179 – 1.♗g6+ ♔g8 [1...♔h8 2.♖e8#] 2.♖e8#
180 – 1.e8♘+ ♔e6 2.d5#
181 – 1.♖xh7+ ♔xh7 [1...♔xh7 2.♘f7#] 2.♖h3#
182 – 1.♖f1 mate with 2.♖f8 is unstoppable
183 – 1.♕h7+ ♔xh7 2.♗f7#
184 – 1.♕b8+ ♔xb8 2.♖d8#
185 – 1.♕f7+ ♗xf7 2.♘d7#
186 – 1.♕g6 ♕xf6 2.♕h7#

The missing piece page 25
187 – 1.♘g6#
188 – 1.♘a4#
189 – 1.♘d3#
190 – 1.♗f7#
191 – 1.♗f6#
192 – 1.♗g4#
193 – 1.♗h6#
194 – 1.♗c6#
195 – 1.♕f6#
196 – 1.♖d5#
197 – 1.♖h6#
198 – 1.♖e7#
199 – 1.h6#
200 – 1.e6#
201 – 1.♗f6#

202 – 1.♖c6#
203 – 1.♕d7#
204 – 1.♗f6#
205 – 1.♖f6#
206 – 1.♗h6#
207 – 1.♖g4#
208 – 1.♘h8#
209 – 1.♕d7#
210 – 1.♖h6#
211 – 1.♘h6#
212 – 1.♖b5#
213 – 1.♖b7#
214 – 1.♗e6+
215 – 1.♘e7+
216 – 1.♖c8

Double attack page 29
217 – 1.♖g6+ ♔f8 2.♖xg4
218 – 1.♘xd7 ♘xd7 2.♕xe6+ e 3.♖xd7
219 – 1.♕g5 threatening both mate on g7 and the ♖ 1...♖g8 [1...♖d7 2.♕f5! threatening both mate on h7 and the ♖ on d7] 2.♕h4 h6 3.♕e4
220 – 1.♕g4 attacking both the ♘ and the ♗
221 – 1.♕d1 attacking both the ♘ and the ♗ on d6. Christiansen–Karpov 1993 1-0
222 – 1.♕c2 attacking both the ♖ and the ♗
223 – 1.♕e4 threatening mate on h7 and the ♗
224 – 1.♕e4! threatening mate on h7 and the ♗
225 – 1.e7+! ♔xe7 2.♘c6+ with an easy win
226 – 1.♖xe2 ♗xe2 2.♕c2 threatening mate and the ♗ on e2 Wojtkiewicz–Privman 2003 1-0
227 – 1.♕e5+ ♔g8 2.♕d5 attacking both ♖s
228 – 1.♖e8+ ♔h7 [1...♗f8 2.♖xf8+! ♔xf8 3.♘f5+ ♔g8 4.♕f8+!! ♔xf8 5.♖d8# Vidmar–Euwe 1929] 2.♕d3+ with the capture of the ♖
229 – 1.♘d5!! ♖c7 forced [1...♖xa4 2.♘e7#] 2.♘xc7 ♘xc7 3.♖c4 with a decisive advantage
230 – 1.d6! ♗xd6 2.♕d2! threatening to win the ♗ or the ♘ if the ♗ moves
231 – 1.♘xd5! a temporary sacrifice 1...cxd5 2.♕a4+ capturing the ♗ with an extra ♙
232 – 1.♗c7! decoy sacrifice 1...♖xc7 2.♕e5! threatening mate on g7 or to capture on c7, thus winning the exchange
233 – 1.♗g8!! threatening mate on h7 and if 1...♕xg8, 2.♖xd8 with a winning position
234 – 1.♕f5!! threatening mate on h7 and if 1...♕xf5 [1...fxg5 2.♕xd7], 2.♘f7#

235 – 1.♕b4! threatening both the ♖ and a winning check with ♕b8+

236 – 1.♕a4 attacking the ♖ on e8 and the ♗

237 – 1.♕g4! Black can't parry the two threats ♕xg7 and 2.♘h6+ with the capture of the ♕

238 – 1.♖e6!! threatening the ♕ and ♕c7 mate

239 – 1.♕b4!! (attacking the ♕and the ♘) 1...♕xb4 2.cxb4 and the ♘ cannot escape capture Maric–Bukal 1973

240 – 1.♕e1! attacking both the ♖ and the ♗

241 – 1.♕b4!! (attacking both the ♕ and the ♗, Morphy–Mongredien 1859) 1...♕c8 [1...♕xb4 2.♖e8+] 2.♕xb7 and wins

242 – 1.♖xf6+ ♕xf6 2.♕e4+ winning the ♖ on a8

243 – 1.♕h1 threatening mate on h7 and the ♗

244 – 1.♕e5! threatening mate on g7 and the ♖

245 – 1.♖f5!! threatening mate on g7 and the capture of the ♕, Plachetka–Peev 1970

246 – 1.♕g5! the e5♗ is now attacked twice with the second threat of ♕xg6 with an easy win

247 – 1.d5! the attack on the ♕ reveals another on the ♘

248 – 1.♘c4! a fork on the ♕ and the ♗

249 – 1.♕g5! threatening mate on g7 and the ♖

250 – 1.♖f5 simultaneous attack on the ♘ and ♗

251 – 1.♖xh8+! allows for a double attack 1...♔xh8 2.♕d4+ winning the ♘

252 – 1.dxc5 and both ♗s are attacked 1...♗xf3 [1...♘xc5 11.♕xg4] 2.cxd6 ♕xd6 3.♘xf3

Discovered attack page 35

253 – 1.g6 (threatening mate and the ♘) 1...hxg6 [1...♘e6 3.♕xh7#] 2.♕xc5 and wins

254 – 1.♘f5 threatening the ♕ and a fork on e7 1...♕e8 2.♘e7+ ♔f7 3.♘xc8 and wins

255 – 1.♖c8! ♖xa7 [1...♖b4 2.a8♕] 2.♔b6

256 – 1.♗f8!! ♖xf8 [1...♖xc1 2.♕xg7#] 2.♖xc8 White has won the exchange

257 – 1.♖xf8+! ♔xf8 2.♗d6+ ♖xd6 3.♕xf5+

258 – 1.♖e7! ♖xe7 [1...g6 2.♖xd7+–] 2.♕h7+ ♔f8 3.♕h8#

259 – 1.♘d5!! ♗xd4 2.♘xe7+ with an extra piece

260 – 1.♖xe7 ♗xe7 2.♕g4 (threatening mate and check on h6) 2...g6 [2...♗f6 3.♕h6+] 3.♕h6+

261 – 1.♕f5+ ♔g8 [1...g6 2.♕xf7#] 2.♘f6+ gxf6 3.♕xd3

262 – 1.♖h6!! Dlugy–Stojko 1991 1-0 1...♕g5 [1...♕xa3 2.♘g6#] 2.♘g6+ ♔xg6 3.♖xg6 hxg6 4.♕e7 the threat ♕h4 can not be stopped

263 – 1.♗b5 ♕xb5 2.♕h3#

264 – 1.♘d6 ♕xg5 [1...♗g6 2.♕xa5] 2.♘f7#

265 – 1.♗e7! and the piece is saved Volchov–Kreslavsky 1970 1-0 1...♘f6 [1...♕xg4 2.♖xd8#] 2.♖xd7 ♘xg4 3.♖xd8+ ♖xd8 4.♗xd8 ♔xd8

266 – 1.♗d1 double attack 1...♕d3 2.♖xf6

267 – 1.f6! ♘xf6 [1...♗xf6 2.♕xf7] 2.♕xe5+ ♔c6 3.♖hxg7 and wins, Smyslov–Kotov 1943

268 – 1.♖xg7! a possible discovered attack on the ♕ makes this move possible 1...♔xg7 2.♖g3+! ♔h7 [2...♔f8 3.♗xh6#] 3.♕c2+ ♔h8 4.♘xf7+ ♖xf7 5.♗xc7, and wins, Nikolenko–Ivanov 1999

269 – 1.♖xf8+! [1.♗h6?! uncer tain after 1...♖xd1+ 2.♔e2 ♘g7 3.♔xd1 e5] 1...♔xf8 2.♗h6+! ♔e8 [2...♖g7 3.g4 and wins] 3.♖xd7 ♔xd7 4.g4 and the ♘ has no squares

270 – 1.♕xc6!! bxc6 [1...♕xd4 2.dxc7+ ♖xc7 3.♕e8+ ♖c8 4.♕xc8+ ♔xc8 5.♗xd4 and wins] 2.♖b4+ winning a piece

271 – 1.♘g5! uncovers the action of the ♗ on g2 and threatens mate on h7 1...fxg5 [1...♗xg2 2.♕xh7#] 2.♗xd5+ winning the ♕

272 – 1.♘xd5 ♖c1 2.♘xe7+ intermediate check 2...♔f8 3.♘g6+! fxg6 4.♔xc1 with a decisive advantage

273 – 1.♕xb8+! ♘xb8 2.♗a3 ♗xb1 [2...♕xa3 3.♖xb8+ ♕f8 4.♖xf8+ and wins] 3.♗xc5 and wins

274 – 1.♘e4! dxe4 2.♖xc6 ♕d5 3.♖xc7

275 – 1.♘e6! ♕xf3 [1...♕xe6 2.♖h3#; 1...♕xe5 2.♖h3+ ♕h5 3.g5#] 2.♕g7#]

276 – 1.♘g5! Prasad–Aaron 1982 1-0 [simpler than 1.♗h7+ ♔xh7 2.♘g5+ ♔g8 3.♘xh3, which also wins] 1...♕xe3 [1...hxg5 2.♕xh3] 2.♗h7+ ♔h8 [2...♔f8 3.♘d7#] 3.♘exf7#

Discovered check page 39

277 – 1.e5+! picking up the ♗ 1...♔c5 2.exd6 ♔xd6 3.♔d3 and wins

278 – 1.♔f6+

279 – 1.♘c3+ winning the ♕

280 – 1.♗f6+ winning ♕
281 – 1.cxd6+ ♔d3 2.dxe7
282 – 1.♖xb4! axb4 2.♘xd5+ ♔d7 [2...♔xd5 3.♖c5#] 3.♘b6+ ♔e7 4.♖c7+ ♔d8 5.♘xa8
283 – 1.♖xb6+ ♔f8 2.♖xb7
284 – 1.♖h8+ ♔xh8 2.♖xg7+ ♔xg7 3.♕xd5
285 – 1.♕xf8! ♖xf8 2.c8♕+
286 – 1.♕xh7+! ♔xh7 2.♗f5+ ♔h6 3.♖xh6#
287 – 1.♘xd4 winning the ♘, if now 1...♕xd4? 2.♗h7+ ♔xh7 3.♖xd4
288 – 1.♘f6+ ♔xf6 2.♘h5+ Petrosian–Stein 1961 1-0 2...♔f7 3.♕h7#
289 – 1.♗xf8+!! ♔xh4 2.♖xf7+ ♔h8 [2...♔g8 3.♗f4+ ♔h7 4.♖xh4#] 3.♗g7+ ♔g8 4.♖xe7+ ♔h7 5.♗f6+ ♔h6 6.♗xh4 and wins
290 – 1.♘e6+ exf4 [1...g5 2.♕f6+ ♕g6 3.♗c1 ♗xe6 4.♗xg5+ ♔h5 5.♗f3+ ♗g4 6.♗xg4+ ♔xg4 7.♗f4+ exf4 8.♕xf4+ ♔h5 9.♕h4#] 2.♗g7#
291 – 1.♘c8+! Kupreichik–Tseshkovky 1976 1-0 1...♘c5 [1...♖c5 2.♕xc5+ ♘xc5 3.♖d8#] 2.♕xc5+ ♕xc5 3.♖d8#]
292 – 1.♖xg7+!! axb5 2.♘f6+ ♔d8 3.♖d7#
293 – 1.♖xh6+ gxh6 2.♘e7+ ♔g7 3.♖xf7 ♔xf7 4.♕xa5 and wins
294 – 1.♖xg6+ fxg6 2.d6+ and wins
295 – 1.♘xg6+ ♕xg6 [1...hxg6 2.♖h3#] 2.♖xc4+ ♕g7 3.♕xg7+ ♔xg7 4.♖c7+ Furman–Smyslov 1949 1-0
296 – 1.♗xh7+ ♔h8 [1...♘xh7 2.♕xd7] 2.♗f5+ a painful discovered check 2...♔g8 3.♗xd7
297 – 1.♘b5+! the ♔ can't protect its ♘
298 – 1.f4+ checks, closes the diagonal, and wins the ♕!
299 – 1.♘h1+ ♔c6 2.♘xf2 and wins
300 – 1.♔b6+!! ♖xg2 2.d8♕+ ♗b8 3.♕d5#

Double check page 43
301 – 1.♕d8+! ♔xd8 2.♗g5+ ♔c7 3.♗d8# Réti–Tartakower 1910
302 – 1.♗f5+! ♔e8 [1...♔c6 2.♗d7#] 2.♗d7+ ♔f8 3.♖xe7# Anderssen–Dufresne 1852
303 – 1.♘f6+ ♔xf6 2.♕d8+ ♔xd8 3.♗b5# double check and mate
304 – 1.♕g7+!! ♔xg7 2.♗f5+ ♔g8 3.♘h6#
305 – 1.♕xh7+ ♔xh7 2.♘f6+ ♔h8 3.♘g6#
306 – 1.♗b5+ ♔f8 [1...♔d8 2.♖e8#] 2.♖e8#
307 – 1.♘g6+ ♔xh7 2.♘xf8+ ♔g8 3.♕h7#

308 – 1.♖xg7+!! ♔xg7 2.♖g5+ the double check can not be dealt with 2...♔f7 3.♖g7+ ♔e8 4.♗g6+ ♖f7 [4...♔d8 5.♕b6+] 5.♕xf4
309 – 1.♗d8+!! elegant double check 1...♔d6 [1...♔xd8 2.♖xg8+ ♔e7 3.♖xa8] 2.♖xg8 and wins
310 – 1.♖e8+! ♖xe8 2.♘c7+ ♔e7 3.♘xd5+ ♖xd5 4.♕xa7+
311 – 1.♕h5!! gxh5 2.♖g3+ ♔h8 3.♘xf7#
312 – 1.♘f6+ ♔f8 2.♗h6#
313 – 1.♖c8+!! ♖xc8 2.♕c5+ ♔d7 3.♕d6+ ♔e8 4.♕e6+ ♔f8 5.♗h6#
314 – 1.♘xf6+ ♔f8 2.♗d6+ ♕xd6 3.♖e8#
315 – 1.♕xg7+! ♔xg7 2.♗g6+ ♔h7 3.♖g7+ ♔h8 4.♖h7+ ♔g8 5.♖h8#
316 – 1.♘xd7+! ♔xe2 [1...♘e6 2.♘f6#] 2.♘f6#
317 – 1.♖c8+ ♔a7 [1...♔xc8 2.♘b6#] 2.♗b8+ ♔a8 3.♘b6#
318 – 1.♕g7+ ♔xg7 2.♖xg6#
319 – 1.♕h7+ ♔xh7 2.♘f6+ ♔h8 3.♖h1#
320 – 1.♕f8+! ♔xf8 2.♗d6+ ♔e8 3.♖f8#
321 – 1.♕xf6+ ♔xf6 2.♘xd5+ ♔g5 3.♗c1+! ♔h5 4.♘f6#
322 – 1.♕f8+ ♔xf8 2.♘e6+ ♔g8 3.♖f8#
323 – 1.♕g7+!! ♔xg7 2.♘f5+ ♔g8 3.♘h6# Mishta–Kloza 1955
324 – 1.♕d8+! ♔xd8 2.♗a5+ ♔c8 [2...♔e8 3.♖d8#] 3.♖d8#

Pin page 47
325 – 1.♘d5+ winning the ♖
326 – 1.♗xc5 the ♙ on d6 is pinned
327 – 1.♕a8#
328 – 1.b4# the ♙ on a4 is pinned
329 – 1.♕xg7# Szekely–Arkhipov 1992
330 – 1.♕f6#
331 – 1.c4 ♘xc4 2.♖xd5+ and wins
332 – 1.♖g1 and White wins the ♗
333 – 1.♖xf6! ♖xf6 2.g5 and wins
334 – 1.♘b5+ ♔c8 [1...♔b8 2.♕a7+ ♔c8 3.♘d6+] 2.♘d6+
335 – 1.♘xb4 cxb4 [1...a5 2.♘d3] 2.♗xb6 with a decisive advantage
336 – 1.♖b1! the pinned ♕ can not capture on b1 1...♕xc5 but there is another relative pin on b7 2.♖xb7#
337 – 1.♕xh7+ ♔xh7 2.♖h5# the pinned ♙ on g6 makes this elegant mate possible

338 – 1.♖d1! winning a ♖ 1...♕xc4 2.♖xd8+ check! 2...♔f7 3.bxc4

339 – 1.♖xe6! ♖xe6 2.b6+! ♔xb6 [2...♔b8 3.♖h8+] 3.♖h6!

340 – 1.♕h4+! ♔g8 2.♕g3+ ♔h8 3.♗c3

341 – 1.♕a3 ♖ac8 2.♖xc5 ♕xc5 [2...♖xc5 4.♖c1] 3.♖c1! ♖xa3 4.♖xc8+ ♔e7 5.bxa3

342 – 1.♖xf6! ♕xf6 2.d6+ (the pinned ♕ cannot capture on d6) 2...♔xd6 3.♕xf6+

343 – 1.♗e6! both pieces are pinned! 1...♗xf3+ is now impossible and e8=♕ is unstoppable

344 – The threat of mate on d1 appears to save Black, but there is ... 1.♕a8!! ♖xa8 2.fxe7 with the lethal threat of ♖d8

345 – 1.♖f1!

346 – 1.♖d7! and mate cannot be stopped

347 – 1.♕xd4! now it seems simple; White wins a piece, Toran–Kuypers 1965 1–0

348 – Black has captured on d4 exploiting the pinned ♘ on f3, but after ...1.♘xd4! ♗xd1 2.♗b5+ ♕d7 3.♗xd7+ ♔xd7 4.♔xd1, White has an extra piece

349 – 1.♖a4 ♘c5 2.b6! ♘xa4 3.b7#

350 – 1.♘xe6!! threatening the ♕ and mate, Bareev–Yakovich 1986 1–0 1...fxe6 [1...♕xh5 2.♘g7+ ♔d8 3.♖e8#] 2.♕xd5 the ♗ is pinned

351 – 1.b5 wins the pinned ♙ on c6, with a decisive advantage

352 – 1.♘g6+! both the ♙ and the ♖ are pinned Bocharov–Babiy 2004 1–0 1...♔g8 [1...♔g8 2.♘xf8] 2.♕xf8+

353 – 1.♗xd5 cxd5 2.♖xc8+ ♗xc8 3.♖xc8+ ♔f7 4.♕xf5+ and wins

354 – 1.♕c4! a double pin 1...♔d6 the lesser of two evils [1...♔f8 2.♖c1] 2.♖d1 ♗d4 3.♖xd4 ♔f8 4.a5 exd4 5.a6 with a decisive advantage

355 – 1.♔e5 defends the ♗ and wins the ♘

356 – 1.♖g8!! ♖xg8 2.♕f6+ ♔e8 3.♕f7+ ♔d8 4.♕xg8+ ♘f8 5.♖xf8+ ♕xf8 6.♕xf8# Schlechter–Teichmann 1908

357 – 1.♖1c6!! ♖xc6 [1...♖xf4 2.♖xd6] 2.dxc6 Wijgerden–Donner 1976 1–0 2...♖xf4 3.cxd7 the promotion will be followed by discovered check

358 – 1.♕f5! it's the ♔ or the ♕ 1...♖xh6 2.♕xf7 ♖c6 3.♔c3 and a theoretically won endgame

359 – 1.♖xf8+! Kortchnoi–Golod 2004 1–0 1...♔xf8 the ♘ is pinned 2.♕xd7

360 – 1.♕g6 with the black pawns on f7 and g7 pinned there will be immediate mate 1...♘xc4 2.♕xg7#

Skewer page 53

361 – 1.♖h7+ ♔e6 2.♖xa7

362 – 1.a8♕+ ♔e3 2.♕xh1

363 – 1.f8♕+ ♔xf8 [1...♖xf8 2.♖xe7+] 2.♖h8+ ♔g7 3.♖xc8

364 – 1.♘xd3 ♖xd3 2.♖a7+ ♔g6 3.♗h7+ ♔g5 4.♗xd3

365 – 1.♘d6+ ♔d5 2.♕f3+ ♔xd6 3.♕xa8 and wins

366 – 1.♗e4! ♕xb7 2.♗xb7 ♘c6 3.♗xa8 and wins

367 – 1.♘e5+ ♔e6 2.♕g8+ ♔d6 3.♕xb3

368 – 1.♕h3!! ♔xf7 to avoid mate after h7 2.♕h7+ ♔e8 3.♕g8+ winning the ♕

369 – 1.♖h8! [1.♖h7?+ ♔f6 2.♖b7 ♗e5] 1...♗c7 2.♖h7+ ♔f6 3.♖xc7

370 – 1.♔f6 ♔e8 [1...♗f7 2.♖c8+ ♔e8 3.♖d8 ♔g8 4.♖xe8+] 2.♖c8+ ♔d7 3.♖xg8

371 – 1.♕e1 ♘g6 2.♗a5 winning the exchange

372 – 1.♕c4+!! ♕xc4 2.g8♕+ winning the ♕

373 – 1.♖xe5! ♖xe5 2.♗xd4 winning the ♖

374 – 1.♖xe4! losing the exchange but winning a ♖.1...♖xe4 2.♗f3

375 – 1.♕g1+!! ♔xg1 2.g8♕+ winning the ♕

376 – 1.e5! [1.♗g3? ♕b6 defending b8] 1...♕xe5 2.♗g3 ♕e3 3.♗xb8 and wins

377 – 1.b7! ♖g8 and the rook has nowhere to go [1...♔a7 2.bxc8♕] 2.♖a8+ ♔xb7 3.♖xg8

378 – 1.♘xe4+!! first a fork 1...dxe4 then a skewer 2.♕d8+

379 – 1.♗e5+ ♔xe5 2.♕c3+ winning the ♕ Short–Vaganian 1989

380 – 1.h7 a2 2.h8♕ a1♕ 3.♕e8+ ♔c5 [3...♔a6 4.♕a8+] 4.♕c8+ ♔b5 5.♕c4+ ♔a5 6.b4+ ♔a4 7.♕a6+ ♔b3 8.♕xa1

381 – 1.e6+! ♔xe6 [1...♔d8 2.♕h8+ ♔e7 3.♕g7+] 2.♕e5+ ♔d7 [2...♔f7 3.♕c7+] 3.♕g7+ ♔c8 4.♕f8+ ♔d7 5.♕f7+ Black must give up the ♕ to avoid mate 5...♔d8 [5...♔c8 6.♕e8#] 6.♕xb7

382 – 1.♖f1 the ♖ on f8 is undefended 1...♕xf1+ [1...♕xg3 2.♖xf8#] 2.♘xf1 and wins

383 – 1.♗d4 ♕e6 2.♗xh8 and wins

384 – 1.♗f4 the ♕ has no square from where it can defend the ♖ and White remains a ♗ up

Deflection page 57

385 – 1.♕a4+! ♕xa4 2.♖c8+ ♖d8 3.♖xd8# Tal-Petrosian 1975

386– 1.♖d8+! ♘xd8 2.♗a7#

387 – 1.♗b7+! ♖xb7 2.♕d5+ ♔f2 3.♕xh1 and wins

388 – 1.♕c7! ♕xc7 2.♗f5#

389 – 1.♕f7! ♖g8 [1...♖xf7 2.♖c8+ and mate] 2.♕xg7+ ♖xg7 3.♖c8+ ♕e8 4.♖xe8#

390 – 1.♗xg5! ♕xf3 2.♗h6#

391 – 1.♗e6!! dxe6 [1...♘h5 2.♗xd7+ ♔xd7 3.♔f8] 2.d7+ ♔xd7 3.♔f8 and promotes

392 – 1.♖f4+! [1.♖h4+?? gxh4 2.♖f4+ ♔h5] 1...gxf4 2.♖h4#

393 – 1.♖xd5! cxd5 2.♗b5 ♕e7 [2...♕xb5 3.♕xg7#] 3.♗xa4 and wins

394 – 1.♖g8+!! ♖xg8 [1...♕xg8 2.♕xd4+ with mate to follow] 2.♕xd4+! ♕xd4 3.♘f7#

395 – 1.♖b6! ♕xb6 2.♕h8+ ♔g6 3.♗h5# Mariotti-Panchenko 1978

396 – 1.♕xe5! Smyslov-Euwe 1953 1-0 1...♕xe5 2.♖xc6+ ♔b8 3.♖b7+ ♔a8 4.♖b5#

397 – 1.♕xe5!! ♕xe5 2.♘xf7+ ♖xf7 3.♖d8+ and mate follows, Capablanca-Fonarov 1918

398 – 1.♕e8+!! ♖xe8 2.♖d7+ ♕xd7 3.♖xd7#

399 – 1.♕xe6 Spassky-Larsen 1969 1-0 1...fxe6 2.f7 ♕b1+ 4.♔h2 and wins

400 – 1.♖a1!! [1.b7 ♔c6 =] 1...♖b4 [1...♖xa1 2.b7 and wins] 2.b7 ♔c5 3.♖a5+ ♔c6 4.♔xb4

401 – 1.e6 ♗f8 [1...♔xc3 2.e7 and promotes] 2.♗g7! ♔xe6 [2...♗xg7 3.e7] 3.♗xf8 and wins

402 – 1.♗d4! 2.♕xh6 and mate cannot be parried with dignity 1...♕b1 [1...♗xd4 2.♕xh6#] 2.♗xg7+! ♖xg7 3.♕xb1 and wins

403 – 1.♘g5+ ♗xg5 2.♖1f7+ ♔h6 3.♖h8#

404 – 1.♖h5!! Skuratov-Svedchikov 1972 1-0 [1.fxe7? ♖xe6] 1...♖xh5 [1...♘g8 2.♖xh6+ ♘xh6 3.e7] 2.fxe7 and promotes

405 – 1.♘d6+! ♗xd6 2.♘xe4

406 – 1.♖e6+ Karpov-Tarjan 1976 1-0 1...fxe6 [1...g6 2.♖xg6+ ♔h7 3.♕xf7+] 2.♕g6#

407 – 1.♕a4! threatening the ♕ and mate on d7 1...♕xa4 2.♖c8#

408 – 1.♖b8! ♕xb8 2.♕xh4 and mate is unstoppable Botvinnik-Keres 1966

Decoy sacrifice page 61

409 – 1.♖c7 ♕xc7 2.♕xh7+ ♔e6 3.♕xc7

410 – 1.♖h8+ ♔xh8 2.♘g6+ ♔g8 [2...♔h7 3.♘e7+] 3.♘e7+ winning the queen

411 – 1.♕f8+ ♔xf8 2.♖d8# Vidmar-Euwe 1929

412 – 1.♕xh6+ ♔xh6 [1...♔g8 2.♕h8#] 2.♖h2#

413 – 1.♗e5+! ♔xe5 2.♕f4+ ♔e6 3.♕xc7

414 – 1.♖xh4 ♕xh4 2.♕xf8+ ♔xf8 3.♘g6+ ♔f7 4.♘xh4 and wins

415 – 1.♕g7+! or 1.♖xh7+ with the same sequence 1...♔xg7 2.fxf7+ ♔g8 3.♗g7+ ♔h8 4.♖h7+ ♔g8 5.♖bg7# PolgarJ.-Hansen 1989

416 – 1.♖d8+!! ♔xd8 2.♕xe4

417 – 1.♕h6+! ♔xh6 [1...♔f7 2.♕f8#] 2.♗f8+ ♔h5 3.g4#

418 – 1.♖c3!! dxc3 [1...♕xb6 2.♖xc8+ and mate in 2; 1...♘e7 2.♖xc6 ♘xc6 3.♕b7 and wins] 2.♕xc6 ♖xc6 3.♖d8+ followed by mate

419 – 1.♕xe6+ ♔xe6 [1...♔e8 2.g6] 2.♗h3#

420 – 1.♗f7+! the most effective, Ni Hua-Wang Zili 2003 1-0 1...♔xf7 [1...♔d8 2.♘e6#] 2.♗xe5+ ♔e8 3.♗xc7

421 – 1.♖h8+!! ♔xh8 2.♗xf7 and there is no power on earth that can prevent ♖h1 and mate

422 – 1.♗f8+!! an elegant deflection of the ♖ from the d file 1...♖xf8 2.♖d3! with mate on h3 to come, Polugaevsky-Szilazy 1960

423 – 1.♕xe8+ ♕xe8 2.♖xc8 ♕xc8 3.♘e7+

424 – 1.♕xc8!! ♕xc8 2.♖xc6 ♕e8 [2...♕xc6 3.♘e7+] 3.♖c8 ♕xc8 4.♘e7+ ♔f8 5.♘xc8

425 – 1.d5+! ♔e5 [1...♔xd5 2.♘c3+; 1...♔f5 2.♘g3+] 2.♕e7+ followed by a ♘fork

426 – 1.♘xg7!! ♔xg7 2.♕xf6+ ♔xf6 3.♘xd5+ ♔g6 4.♘xc7 and wins

427 – 1.♗xe6+! a thunderbolt out of the blue 4...♔xe6 2.♕f8+ ♔xf8 3.♘xe6+ ♔e7 4.♘xc7 ♔d6 5.♘e8+ Seirawan-Kogan 1986 1-0

428 – 1.a4! ♖xa4 2.♗a3 ♗b5 3.♖xb5 the black ♕ is hanging 3...♖xa3 4.♖b7+ intermediate check 4...♔g8 5.bxa3 and White has an extra piece

429 – 1.♗xf7+! ♔xf7 2.♘e6! threatening the ♕ 2...♔xe6? [after 2...♔g8 3.♘xc7 ♖b8 White is better but Black can defend] 3.♕d5+ ♔f6 4.♕f5#

430 – 1.♕xh7+!! ♔xh7 2.♘xf6+ ♔h6 [2...♔h8?? 3.♘g6#] 3.♘eg4+ ♔g5 4.h4+ ♔f4 5.g3+ ♔f3 6.♗e2+ [6.0-0 ♔xf6 7.♗e2+] 6...♔g2 7.♖h2+ ♔g1 8.0-0-0# Lasker Ed.-Thomas 1912

431 – 1.♕xg7+ ♔xg7 2.♘xd7+ ♔g8 3.♘f6+ ♔f7 4.♘d5+ Keres-Spassky 1955 1-0 2...♔g8 3.♘f6+ ♔f7 4.♘d5+

432 – 1.♘f7! (a pleasing decoy sacrifice)

1...♔xf7 [1...♕f6 2.fxg5 and wins] 2.fxg5+ and Black loses the ♕

Promotion page 65

433 – 1.♘b5 and the ♙ promotes

434 – 1.b8=♖! [1.b8=♕?? stalemate]

435 – 1.♗b7 the ♗ sacrifices itself so the ♙ can promote on the next move

436 – 1.f7 ♗c5 2.♗d4! pinning the ♗ so the ♙ can promote 2...♗xd4 [2...♔b7 3.♗xc5] 3.f8=♕

437 – 1.♘d7! denying access to b6 [1.a7?? ♔b7 2.♘c6 ♔a8 theoretical draw: when the White ♔ approaches it is stalemate] 1...♔c6 [1...♔xd7 2.a7] 2.♔b2 ♔c7 3.♔c3 ♔c6 4.♔d4 ♔c7 5.♔d5 ♔c8 6.♔d6 and mate in 4

438 – 1.♖c8+! ♖xc8 2.♖xc8+ ♔xc8 3.bxa7

439 – 1.♖xb6! axb6 2.a7 and promotes

440 – 1.♗h7! if the ♗ does not control the queening square, if the ♔ can reach the corner it is a draw 1...♔f8 2.♔g4 ♔f7 3.♔f5 ♔f8 5.♔f6 ♔e8 6.♗f5 ♔f8 7.h7 mate next move

441 – 1.♔e8! g2 2.♔d8 g1♕ 3.♗xc7#

442 – 1.c7 ♖xe6 [1...♔d7 2.♖xe7+] 2.c8=♕+

443 – 1.♕h8+!! making way for the ♙ 1...♔xh8 2.g7+ ♔g8 3.♗h7+! ♔xh7 4.g8=♕#

444 –1.♖b5!! closing the file to protect the ♙ 1...axb5 [1...cxb5 2.b7] 2.b7 ♖xa5 3.b8=♕+ ♔d7 4.♕b7+ and wins

445 –1.♖f8+! ♔xf8 2.e7a typical endgame tactic: the ♙ attacks the ♘ and then promotes 2...♔xe7 and now the ♙ promotes

446 – 1.axb6! ♕xb3 2.bxa7 ♕xb2 3.a8♕ ♕xc3 4.♗d6 and wins

447 – 1.♖d8+ ♖xd8 2.♖f8+ ♔xf8 3.cxd8♕+

448 – 1.g8=♗! a promotion to ♕ or ♖ is immediate stalemate 1...♔g1 2.♘e2+ ♔g2 3.♗d5#

449 – 1.♖xg7+!! the quickest and most elegant 1...♘xg7 2.h6 and the ♙ promotes 2...♖g4 3.h7

450 – 1.♘e6! controlling g7 and promotion is guaranteed 2...♗b3 [2...♔xe6 3.h7] 3.h7

451 – 1.e7 ♘xe7 2.d6 ♔f8 [2...♘d5 3.d7; 2...f5 3.d7] 3.d7 and wins: the ♙ on c6 prevents ♘c6 and the ♘ on e7 keeps the ♔ at bay

452 – 1.♘f7 does the trick: threatening mate 1...♖xf7 2.♖h8+!! the point of the exercise! [2.gxf7+? ♔xf7 and Black wins] 2...♔xh8 3.gxf7 the ♙ promotes and White wins

453 – 1.♖f5!! the idea is the advance to g4 vacating the g2 square 1...♔xf5 2.g4+ ♔xg4 3.♔g2 the

endgame with 3 ♙s to 2 is winning for White

454 – 1.g5 ♔xf5 [1...fxg5 2.f6] 2.gxh6 and the ♔ cannot approach: if there were not a ♙ on f6, the ♔ could move to f6 with a draw 2...c2 3.♔d2 ♔g5 4.h7

455 – 1.exf6! ♖xg7 2.fxg7 and promotes

456 – 1.♕xa7! ...♖xa7 2.bxa7 and the ♙ with a decisive advantage 2...♘c2+ 3.♔d2 ♘xa1 4.♖xa1 0–0 5.a8♕

457 – 1.g8=♕+! the simplest: the resulting pawn endgame is winning for White 1...♕xg8 2.♕xg8+ ♔xg8 3.b4 Svidler–Dreev 2004 1–0 3...♔h7 4.a4 ♔xh6 5.b5

458 – 1.♖e8+ ♔xe8 [1...♗f8 2.♖xf8+! ♕xf8 3.f7+ ♕g7 4.f8♕#] 2.f7+ ♕e5 3.♗xe5+ ♔xe5 4.f8=♕#

459 – 1.♕xe4+! [1.gxh7? ♗xh7 and Black is better] 1...dxe4 2.gxh7 and wins

460 – 1.♔f7 threatening to capture the ♙ 1...h5 2.♔e6 h4 3.♔d5 h3 [3...♔b3 4.♔e4] 4.♔c4 h2 5.♗b4! h1♕ 6.b3# study by Fritz 1939

461 – 1.♗g2! h1♕ [1...♕xg2 2.♖c8#] 2.♖c8♕#

462 – 1. ♘a6+! a rare ♔ + ♘ fork! (the immediate 1.♔e7? is a blunder: after 1...♘c6+ the queening square is controlled) 1...♘xa6 2.♔e7 and now that the black ♘ has been deflected to a6, promotion is inevitable

463 – 1.a6 the ♔ can enter the square and Black has a ♘, but still the ♙ promotes ! 1...♔c7 [1...♘c5 2.a7] 2.a7 it is the very presence of the ♘ that prevents the ♔ from approaching !

464 – 1.♔h5! controls g6 and threatens ♘g4+ and h7 1...♔xe5 2.h7 with promotion

465 – 4.h3!! mate in 16! [4.h4+? ♔h5 zugzwang] 4...♔h5 5.h4 zugzwang [5.♔xg8?? ♔xh6 draw] 5...♔xh4 [5...♔b3 6.h7] 6.♔xg8

466 – 1.♗e4!! again the Novotny theme: Black cannot maintain control of both a8 and e8 1...♕exe4 [1...♕hxe4 2.e8♕+ ♕xe8 (2...♔b7 3.a8♕#) 3.a8♕#] 3.a8♕+ ♕xa8 5.e8♕+ ♔b7 6.♕xd7+ ♔b8 7.♕c7#

467 – 1.c5!! not at all easy to find: by not advancing to the 7th rank White gains the ♘ or the ♖! Stopping ♘d6 threatens c7 [1.c7? ♘d6 2.c5 ♘c8 3.axb3 ♔f7 and Black wins; 1.axb3? ♘d6] 1...♖b5 [1...♘xc5 2.c7 and promotes; 1...♖e3 2.cxb7 ♖e8 3.c6] 2.a4!! taking the ♖ away from the key b5 square 2...♖xc5 [2...♘xc5 3.c7] 3.cxb7 and b5 is controlled

468 – The final part of the celebrated study by Saavedra of 1895 1.c8♖!! threatening mate on a8 [1.c8♕? ♖c4+! 2.♕xc4 stalemate] 1...♖a4 forced 2.♔b3 threatening the ♖ and mate on c1

Drawing tactics page 71

469 – 1.♖c4+! ♕xc4 stalemate

470 – 1.♖d3+! ♕xd3 stalemate

471 – 1.♖h3+!! ♔xh3 stalemate

472 – 1.♖c1! ♕xc1 stalemate

473 – 1.♖xb2! ♖h2+ 2.♔f3 ♖xb2 stalemate [2...♖h3+ draw] Bernstein–Smyslov 1946

474 – 1.♗d3+! ♗xd3 stalemate

475 – 1.♖f5!! [1.♖xb5+? axb5! 2.♔g5 b4 and Black wins] 1...♔xf5 stalemate[1...♔c5? 2.♖xc5+ bxc5 3.♔g5 White wins]

476 – 1.♕a5+ ♔b8 2.♕d8+ ♔a7 3.♕a5+ draw by perpetual check

477 – 1.♘g6+ ♔g8 2.♘e7+ ♔h8 3.♘g6+ draw by perpetual check

478 – 1.♕g2+!! ♖xg2 stalemate; a study by Kubbel

479 – 1.♖b5!! c1♕ 2.♖c5+ ♕xc5 draw

480 – 1.♕f4+!! ♕xf4 stalemate

481 – 1.♕g8+!! ♔xg8 stalemate

482 – 1.♕f2+ ♔xf2 stalemate

483 – 1.♔g1!! [1.♕xf6?? ♘e4+] 1...♘f3+ [1...♖xf4 stalemate!] 2.♕xf3+ ♖xf3 stalemate

484 – 1.h8♕+ ♔e4 2.♕h1+!! ♕xh1 stalemate

485 – 1.♕g5+!! ♔xg5 stalemate

486 – 1.♗f2+!! ♕xf2 stalemate; a study by Stromberg

487 – 1.♕g3+!! ♔xg3 stalemate; a study by Mikhalap

488 – 1.♗d5+ ♔h7 2.♗e4+ ♔g8 3.♗d5+ perpetual check

489 – 1.♗f3!! [1.♗xa8 ♔xa8 2.♔f2 ♔b8 3.♔e3 ♔c7 and a winning pawn endgame for Black] 1...♕xf3 stalemate; a study by Dawson

490 – 1.g5 it is hard to get this wrong; it is the only legal move!1...hxg5 stalemate [1...♗xg5 theoretical draw]

491 – 1.g7 only legal move 1...♖xg7 stalemate

492 – 1.♕f1+! ♖xf1 stalemate

Mixed motifs: White page 75

493 – 1.♗e2#

494 – 1.♕xh7+ ♔xh7 2.♖h4#

495 – 1.♕xg5+ ♔f8 [1...♘g6 2.♕h6] 2.♕g7+ ♔e8 3.♕g8+ ♔d7 4.♗h3+ and mate

496 – 1.♗f3+!! ♖xf3 2.♕e4+! ♕xe4 3.♖c8#

497 – 1.♕xc8! ♖xc8 2.♘d7+ ♔e8 3.♘xb6 with a decisive advantage

498 – 1.♕xf6+!! wins for White! 1...♔xf6 2.♘e4+ ♔f5 3.♘xd2

499 – 1.♗e4+ ♔e6 2.♗d5+! ♔xd5 [2...♕xd5 3.♘c7+] 3.♘c3+

500 – 1.♗d5! skewer and decoy 1...♕xd5 2.♘e7+ ♔f7 3.♘xd5

501 – 1.♘h6+ ♔h8 2.♘f7+ ♔g8 3.♘h6+ perpetual check

502 –1.♘xe5!! ♗xd1 [1...dxe5 2.♕xg4 with a decisive advantage] 2.♗xf7+ ♔e7 3.♗d5#

503 –1.♘e6+ fxe6 [1...♔h6 2.♖xf6 fxe6 3.♖c7] 2.♖c7+ ♔h6 3.♕xf6 with mate to follow

504 – 1.♗f7+ ♔xf7 [1...♔f8 2.♗xg6] 2.e6+ ♔xe6 3.♕xa5

505 – 1.♘bc5+! bxc5 2.♘xc5+ ♔c6 3.♘xe4

506 – 1.♖h8! threatens to promote, creating a lethal skewer 1...♖xa7 2.♖h7+ ♔e6 3.♖xa7

507 –1.♗d6!! with an eye on e7 1...♕e1 the ♗ threatens a double attack or mate on g3; Black has no good moves and can no longer maintain the pin on the ♙ on g2 . [1...g4 2.♗e7+ ♕f6 3.♗xf6#] 2.g3+ ♕xg3+ 3.♗xg3#

508 – 1.♘h6+ ♔h8 2.♘xe5! ♕xe5 3.♘xf7+ ♖xf7 [3...♔g8 4.♘xe5 with a decisive advantage] 4.♖d8+ with mate in 2

509 – 1.♗xh6! gxh6 2.♖xh6+ ♔g7 3.♗b7!! freeing the diagonal 3...♕xh6 [3...♕xb7 4.♕g6#] 4.♗xa6 and wins

510 – 1.♖xe6!! fxe6 2.♕xf8+!! decoy sacrifice 2...♔xf8 3.♘xe6+ ♔e7 4.♘xc7 and wins

511 – 1.♗g7+! more effective than 1.♖g7 1...♕xg7 [1...♘xg7 2.♕xh7#] 2.♖xg7 and wins

512 –1.b5 ♗xb5 2.♘cd6+ ♘xd6 3.♘xd6+ ♔e6 4.♘xb5 and wins

513 – 1.♖xg7+!! ♔xg7 2.♕xd4+! ♕xd4 3.♘xe6+ ♔f6 4.♘xd4 with a decisive advantage

514 – 1.♕xf6! ♘xf6 2.d8♕+ ♔a7 3.♕xf6 with a decisive advantage

515 – 1.♘e7+ ♔h8 2.♖xh7+!! ♔xh7 3.♖h4#

516 – 1.♖xc6+! decoy sacrifice 1...♕xc6 2.♘e7+ ♔c7 3.♘xc6 ♔xc6 White wins

517 – 1.g4!...fxg4 2.f5 gxf5 [2...♔e5 3.fxg6] 3.g6 hxg6 4.h7 and wins!

518 – 1.Re7 Qxe7 2.Qxd5+ Ne6 3.Qxa8+

519 – 1.Rxg7+! Kxg7 2.Ne6+ Kf7 3.Nxc7

520 – 1.Nh6+ Kh8 2.Nf7+ Kg8 3.Nh6+ draw

521 – 1.Rf6+!! Qxf6 2.e5+ Kxe5 [2...Qxe5 3.Nf7+] 3.Ng4+ and wins

522 – 1.Qa4+!! Qxa4 2.Nc7+ Kf8 3.Rxd8+

523 – 1.e6! threatens the fork on f7 and the N on d7 1...Bxe6 2.Bxe6 Rxe6 3.Rxd7

524 – 1.Qf8+! Kxf8 2.Rh6+ Kg8 3.Re8#

525 – 1.Nc7 Bb7 2.Ne8!! Ng8 3.Nxd6+

526 – 1.Rxg7+! Kxg7 2.Bh6+! Kxh6 3.Qg5#

527 – 1.Qb7!! Rc8 [1...Qxb7 2.Rxd8#] 2.Rxd8+ Qxd8 3.Qxa7 with a winning position

528 – 1.Bc5! Rxd3 [1...Bxc5 2.Rxd8#] 2.Bxe7+ Ke8 3.cxd3 and wins

529 – 1.Rc5! Qa3 [1...Rb5 2.Qe3+ Kg7 3.Qe5+ f6 4.Rxb5] 2.Rh5+!! gxh5 3.Qf6#

530 – 1.Rxc6! bxc6 2.Rb1+ Ka8 3.Qxc8#

531 – 1.Rc8+! Rxc8 2.Qxa7+!! Kxa7 3.bxc8N+! and with three extra Ps White wins

532 – 1.Rd8+ Kb7 2.Rb8+! Kxb8 3.Rc6+

533 – 1.Nd4!! Kxd4 [1...g1Q 2.Ne2+] 2.b8Q g1Q 3.Qxa7+

534 – 1.Bxe5!...Rxe5 2.Qxe5 dxe5 3.Bxe6 the P on f7 is pinned

535 – 1.Ng4+!! hxg4 [1...Kg7 2.Qxg5] 2.Rh1+ Kg7 3.Qxg5

536 – 1.Qxf6! gxf6 2.Ne7+ Kg7 3.Nxd5

537 – 1.Bh6+! Kxh6 2.Qd2+ Kg7 3.Nxd8

538 – 1.Rxg6+! [1.Bxc5+? Kxc5 2.Rxg6 Rf3] 1...hxg6 2.Bxc5+ Kxc5 3.Kxd3

539 – 1.Rxe5+!! fxe5 [1...Nxe5 2.Qd8#] 2.Qd8+ Nxd8 3.Rxd8#

540 – 1.Qf8+! deflection 1...Rxf8 2.Ng7+ double check 2...Kd8 3.Re8#

541 – 1.Qe8+ Qf8 2.Rh8+ Kxh8 3.Qxf8+

542 – 1.Re8+!! Rxe8 2.Qg4+! Qg5 [2...Qxg4 3.Nf6#] 3.Qxf5 and wins

543 – 1.Qg4+! Qxg4 2.Rxe8+ Kg7 3.fxg4

544 – 1.Qc3! and both Rs are attacked; if 1...Rbh4 2.Qxc8+ Rxc8 3.Rxc8#

545 – 1.Bg5!! Bxf3! 2.Qc1!! [2.Qd2 Bb4!] 2...Qxd4 3.Qc8+ Qd8 4.Qxd8#

546 – 24.Bxb7+! winning the Q 24...Kxb7 25.Nc5+

547 –1.Qh8+ Rxh8 2.Nf6#

548 – 1.Rd8+!! Rxd8 [1...Kg7 2.Rxc8; 1...Qxd8 2.Qe5+] 2.Qc3+ with mate to follow

549 – 1.Qh6+ gxh6 2.Rh7#

550 – 1.Qxe5+!! dxe5 2.Re6#

551 – 1.Rxc6+! Rxc6 2.Qb4#

552 –1.Bd5! cxd5 2.Rxe6

553 – 1.Rd7!! Tiviakov–Nyback 2005 1-0 1...Qxd7 [1...Nxd7 2.Qxb7#] 2.Rxd7 and wins

554 – 1.Bd3! with attacks on the Q and the R on c8 1...Qxd3 [1...Rxc1 2.Bxg6 Rxe1+ 3.Qxe1 fxg6 4.Bxf6 and wins.] 2.Rxc8+ with a decisive advantage

555 – 1.Qxh6! gxh6 2.Bh7#

556 – 1.Rxh6+!! Bxh6 [1...Kxh6 2.Qh4#] 2.Qxc3

557 – 1.Qxh7+! Kxh7 2.Rh5+ Kg8 3.Rh8#

558 – 1.Qf6+ Kg7 2.h6 Rbg8 3.Rh1!

559 – 1.Rxg5 fxg5 2.Qxh7+ Qxh7 3.Rxh7#

560 – 1.Qe5! attacking both black Rs 1...Rxb5 [1...Kf7 32.Rf6+] 2.Qxh8+ Kd7 3.Rd6+ Kxd6 4.Qxd8+ and wins

561 – 1.g4 unleashing an attack on the Q with the threat of mate on c8. Luchowski–Gridnew Moscow 1992 1...Bxf3 [1...h5 2.Qxh3] 2.Rc8+ Re8 3.Rxe8#

562 – 1.Qxh7+ Kxh7 2.Rh4#

563 – 1.Bb5 MacDonnell–Bird London 1872 1...c6 [1...Rh8 2.Qe7#] 2.Qc7#

564 – 1.Nh7+ Kxh7 2.Rf7#

565 – 1.Nf5+! Kg5 [1...gxf5 2.Qxf6+ Kh5 3.Be2#] 2.Nxd6 Qxe6+ 3.dxe6 and wins

566 – 1.g6! threatening g7 and freeing the R 1...fxg6 [1...Ra7 2.g7; 1...Kxg6 2.Rg8+; 1...Ra7 2.Rxa7 Bxa7 3.g7] 2.Rf8+ Bxf8 3.a8Q

567 –1.Qf6+! Topalov–Naiditsch 2005 1-0 1...Qxf6 2.Re8+ Qf8 3.Rxf8#

568 – 1.Qb7 making way for the P 1...Ke6 2.c7

569 – 1.Qb3+! Rxb3 [1...Kh8 2.Rxh7#] 2.Rg7+ Kh8 3.Rxh7+ Kg8 4.Rag7#

570 – 1.Rg8+! decoy sacrifice 1...Kxg8 2.Ne7+ Kg7 3.Nxf5+ Rxf5 4.Qxb7 and wins

571 – 1.Rh7+!! Kxh7 2.Bf5+ Kg7 3.Bxe4 Bxe4 4.Rxd8

572 – 1.Rxb4!! Qxb4 2.Qxf6+! Kxf6 3.Nd5+ Ke5 4.Nxb4 with a decisive advantage

573 – 1.Bxg7+ Kxg7 2.Qxd6!! Qxd6 3.Nf5+ Kf6 4.Nxd6

574 – 1.Nh6+ Kh8 2.Qxd8 Qxd8 3.Nf7+ Kg8 4.Nxd8 with a decisive advantage

575 – 1.Bf7+ interfering with the defence of the

♙ on g7 1...♔xf7 [1...♗xf7 2.♕xg7#] 2.♖xf7 ♔xf7 3.♕xg7+ ♔e6 4.♖e3+ and mate follows

576 – 1.e5! dxe5 2.♘xc6 ♗xc6 3.♗d5 ♘xd5 [3...♕xd2 4.♘xe7#] 4.♖xa5

577 – 1.♖f8!! ♕xf8 [1...♕xe5 2.c3#; 1...♕h3 2.c3+ ♔xe5 3.f4#] 2.♘f6!! gxf6 [2...♕a8 3.♘d7 ♕f3 4.c3#; 2...♕c8 3.f4 gxf6 4.c3#; 2...♕b8 3.c3+ ♔xe5 4.♘d7+ ♔d6 5.♖xb8 ♗c7 6.♘xa6+ ♔b6 7.♘xc5 ♔xc5 8.♔c2 e5 9.♔b3 and wins] 3.f4!! fxe5 4.c3#

578 – 1.♖g8+! ♔h7 2.♕g6+!! fxg6 3.fxg6+ ♔xg8 4.f7#

579 – 1.♗g5!! [1.♔g6?? g1♕+] 1...g1♕ [1...fxg5 2.♔g6 the ♙ on g5 shields White's ♔] 2.♗xf6+ ♕g7 3.♗xg7+ ♔g8 4.♗d4 and mate

580 – 1.♘d7+ ♔c8 2.♘b6+ ♔b8 3.♕c8+ ♖xc8 4.♘d7#

581 – 1.♖a8+!! ♔xg7 2.♔c6 the black ♖ has no escape square! 2...♖b5 3.♖xb5 d3 4.♖d8 e4 5.♔c4 ♔f6 6.♔d4 ♔f5 7.♔e3 and wins

582 – 1.♖xe6+ ♔xe6 2.♘hg5+! hxg5 3.♘xg5+ ♔f6 4.♖xh7+ ♔g6 5.♘f8+ ♔f7 6.♘d7 and wins

583 – 1.♖h8+ the historic Damiano's mate 1...♔xh8 2.♖h1+ ♔g8 3.♖h8+ ♔xh8 4.♕h1+ ♖h5 5.♕xh5+ ♔g8 6.♕h7#

584 – 1.♗xf5+! exf5 [1...♔g7 2.♕g6+] 2.♖e7+ with mate to follow. Arik–Van Wely 2005 1–0

585 – 1.♕d2!! a nice cross pin: Robach–Jansa Sochi 1974 1–0 [also 1.♕e1! with the same idea is winning]

586 – 1.♕a8+ ♔h7 2.♕e4+ ♔h8 3.♕a8+ ♔h7 4.♕e4+ g6 5.♕xg6+ ♔h8 6.♕xh6+ ♔g8 7.♕g6+ ♔h8 draw

587 – 1.♕xg7+! the most effective 1...♔xg7 2.fxe8♘+! safer than a ♕ promotion, though this is still winning 2...♔f8 3.♘xc7 ♔e7 4.♖d1 with an extra ♖

588 – 1.♗xc6 bxc6 2.♖xh7+ ♕xh7 3.♕xf6+ ♕g7 4.♕xd8+

589 – 1.♕xh6+! gxh6 2.g7+ ♔h7 3.gxf8♘+! ♔h8 4.♖g8#

590 – 1.♗xh7+! ♔xh7 2.♕h4+ [2.♘g5+? ♔g6] 2...♔g8 [2...♔g6 3.♕g5+] 3.♘g5 ♖fe8 4.♕h7+ ♔f8 5.♕h8+ ♔e7 6.♕xf7+

591 – 1.♕g8+!! ♔xg8 [1...♖xg8 2.♘f7#] 2.♘e7+ ♔h8 3.♘f7+ ♖xf7 4.♖xc8+ ♖f8 5.♖xf8#

592 – 1.♘d6+ ♗xd6 2.♖xd7+ ♔e7 3.♖xe7+ ♔xe7 4.♘c6+ ♔d6 5.♘xb8 and wins

593 – 1.♕xf7+!! ♘xf7 2.♘g6#

594 – 1.♗g3! ♖xg3 2.b8♕ and wins

595 – 1.♘f6+! interfering with the defence of f8 1...♕xf6 [1...gxf6 2.♕xf8#] 2.gxf6

596 – 1.♖g2!! breaking the pin. 1...♕xf3 [1...♖c8 2.♖h3 with mate on h7; 1...♖g8 2.♖xh7+ ♔xh7 3.♖h3#] 2.♕xf8# Sultanbeev–Colle 1928

597 – 1.♖c4!! ♖xc4 [1...♖xd2 2.♖c8#] 2.♕xb2 with a winning position

598 – 1.♖xb7 ♖xb7 2.c6+

599 – 1.♕xf6+! gxf6 2.♗xh6#

600 – 1.♕h6! ♗xh6 [1...♖xd4 2.♘e7+ ♔h8 3.♕xf8#] 2.♖xh6#

601 – 1.♖e8+! ♗xe8 [1...♖xe8 2.♕g7#] 2.♕e7#

602 – 1.a7 ♗xa7 2.♔c8 winning the ♗ Larsen–Miles 1–0

603 – 1.f4! axb3 [1...d4 2.♘d2#] 2.♘d2#

604 – 1.♕xf8+!! decoy sacrifice 1...♔xf8 2.♘g6+ a pin and ♘ fork

605 – 1.♕xb8+!! ♘xb8 2.♖d8#

606 – 1.♖xg5+ hxg5 2.♗xd2

607 – 1.♖xf4! exf4 2.♗h8! and mate on g7

608 – 1.♕xf6 ♖xc8 [1...♕xf6 2.♖xe8+ ♖f8 3.♖xf8#] 2.♕xd4

609 – 1.♘xe5 ♖xe5 2.f4

610 – 1.♘c3 ♕d6 2.♘e4

611 – 1.♗d6!! annulling the protection of f8 1...♗xd6 [1...♖7xd6 2.♖e8+ ♕f8 3.♖xf8#] 2.♕xd3 with a winning position

612 – 1.♕c8+! ♗xc8 2.♖e8#

613 – 1.♕g8+!! ♘xg8 2.♗f5#

614 – 1.♖xg5 fxg5 2.gxh7 and promotes

615 – 1.♘g6!! Black is up the exchange and has a 3 ♙ plus, but now both the ♕ and mate are threatened 1...♕xh2 [1...fxg6 2.♕xe5 with a decisive advantage] 2.♘de7#

616 – 1.♕xd4+ ♖xd4 2.b6#

617 – 1.♖d8+ ♔f7 [1...♔h7 2.♖h8#] 2.♖f8#

618 – 1.♗d5 with a double attack on the 2 ♘s

619 – 1.b4+ ♔d5 2.e4+

620 – 1.♖e4!! threatening 2. ♖xe8# or 2. ♕xf6#

621 – 1.♔c6! threatening the ♖ and mate on e8

622 – 1.♗c4+!! clearing the diagonal: 2.♕h7# follows

623 – 1.♘a3 and after 2.♗c3 the ♘ is doomed

624 – 1.♘f5! threatening the ♕ and mate on h8

625 – 1.b5! if the ♘ flees there will be a fork on e7

626 – 1.♖e5 with a double attack on ♗ and ♘

627 – 1.♖g8#

628 – 1.♗e5!! Miles−Pritchett 1982, 1−0. both g7 and e8 cannot be defended

629 – 1.♖e8+! ♔g7 [1...♖xe8 2.♕xd5+] 2.♖xd8

630 – 1.♖d8+!! ♖xd8 [1...♔xd8 2.♕e8#] 2.♕xb7

631 – 1.♕xh6+ gxh6 2.♖h7#

632 – 1.♕b8+! ♘xb8 2.♖f8#

633 – 1.♘a5!! there is the threat of mate and the ♕ is attacked 1...bxa5 [1...♔xa5 2.♖a8#] 2.♖xb3

634 – 1.♖xg7+ ♔xg7 2.♗xh3

635 – 1.♕e4 threatening mate on h7 and the ♗

636 – 1.♖e1! and either the ♘ or ♗ is lost

637 – 1.♕d1+!! ♕xd1 and White is without a move!

638 – 1.♘b6+ ♔b8 [1...axb6 2.♕a8#] 2.♘xd5

639 – 1.0−0−0!! winning a piece

640 – 1.♗a6!! stops the ♙ from advancing 1...bxa6 with a rook's ♙ and ♗ of the wrong colour it is a draw: the White ♔ goes back and forth in the promotion corner and when the ♙ arrives on a2 there is stalemate [1...♔c7 2.♗xb7 is a theoretical draw]

641 – 1.h5 ♘h4 2.h6 winning the ♗

642 – 1.♖xg7+! ♔xg7 2.♕f7+ ♔h8 3.♕h7#

643 – 1.♖g4! ♕xg4 all other moves lose the ♕ 2.♕xf7+ ♔h8 3.♕xh7#

644 – 1.f7+ ♗xf7 2.♕h7#

645 – 1.g6!! the space advantage allows a forced promotion 1...hxg6 [1...fxg6 2.h6 gxh6 3.f6] 2.f6! gxf6 3.h6

646 – 1.♘h6! ♕xh3 [1...gxh6 2.♕xe6; 1...♖e7 2.♕xe6 ♖xe6 3.♘f7+ ♔g8 4.♘xd8] 2.♘xf7+ intermediate check 2...♔g8 3.gxh3 with a decisive advantage

647 – 1.♖xd7+! decoy sacrifice! 1...♔xd7 2.♘e5+ ♔e6 3.♘xg6

648 – 1.♗xh7+! ♘xh7 2.♘g6 the black ♕ is trapped

649 – 1.♗xf7+! vacating a square 1...♖xf7 2.♘c4 with the capture of the ♕

650 – 1.♗f8!! ♖xf8 [1...♕xd5 2.♕g7#; 1...♕c1+ 2.♔h2 changes nothing] 2.♘e7#

651 – 1.♗xb7!! ♗xb7 2.♘e6+

652 – 1.♖c6+!! bxc6 2.♗xa6#

653 – 1.d5! ♘e5 2.♕a4+ winning the ♘ on e4

654 – 1.♘e6! threatening mate on f8 and the

♘ on e4 1...♖xd7 [1...♕xe6 2.♘f8#] 2.♕xe4+ f5 3.♕xf5#

655 – 5.♗f5+ ♔h8 6.♘e5 threatening mate on f7 6...♖h7 7.♘g6#

656 – 1.♕g5+ ♔f8 2.♕d8+ ♔g7 3.♕g5+ perpetual check

657 – 1.♕e7!! ♗xe7 2.dxe7+ ♔c8 3.♖a7

658 – 1.♖e7!! ♘xe7 [1...♕xe7 2.fxe7 ♘xe7 3.♖d8 and wins.] 2.♕xf8+ ♔xf8 3.♖d8#

659 – 1.♕e8+ ♗f8 2.♕xf7+ ♔h8 3.♕xh7# [3.♕xf8#]

660 – 1.♘d5! attacking the ♕ 1...♕xd2 2.♘xe7+ check! 2...♔h8 3.♘xd2 with an extra piece

661 – 1.♕a7!! [1.♕c5? ♖xd5!] 1...♖xa7 [1...♖d5 2.♕xa8+ ♕d8 3.♕xd8+ ♖xd8 4.♖xd8#] 2.♖xd8+ ♕xd8 3.♖xd8#

662 – 1.♘e4!! and both the ♕ and ♖ are hanging [1.♕f8+?? ♖xf8 the ♖ on f1 is pinned] 1...♕xe4 [1...♖xe4 2.♕f8#] 2.♕f8+ ♔xf8 3.♖xf8#

663 – 1.♘h6+ ♔h8 2.♕g8+ ♖xg8 3.♘f7#

664 – 1.♗xf7!! ♖xf7 [1...♕xd4 2.♘g6#] 2.♘g6+ ♔g8 3.♘xe5

665 – 1.♕xh5 opening the diagonal 1...gxh5 [1...f6 2.♕g6+ ♕g7 3.♘xe6] 2.♗h7#

666 – 1.♖xg5! fxg5 2.♗e5

667 – 1.♕h7+! ♘xh7 2.♗xh7#

668 – 1.♕h5+ ♔g8 2.♗xe8+

669 – 1.♘xc6 ♖xd1+ 2.♖xd1 winning back the ♕ the exchange up

670 – 1.♔c2 ♖xc4 2.♖e1#

671 – 1.♘e5+ winning a piece 1...♗xe5 2.♗xg4+

672 – 1.♗e5+!! ♘xe5 2.♕g5#

673 – 1.♗xd5 ♗xd5 [1...cxd5 2.♖xa6] 2.♕xf6+

674 – 1.b4!! decoy sacrifice 1...♗xb4 2.♘c2 threatening both the ♗ and the ♘

675 – 1.h8♖ with the threat of mate to follow on h6 [1.h8♕?? ♖d8+ 2.♕xd8 stalemate] 1...♖d6 [1...♖d7 2.♖h6+ ♔d6 3.♖xd6#] 2.♖c7 either Black loses the rook or it's mate. 1924 study by Troitzky

676 – 1.e7+ ♕xe7 [1...♖xe7 2.♕h8#] 2.♕h8#

677 – 1.♗d2!! ♗c5 [1...♗xd2 2.♖e7#] 2.♖xa5

678 – 1.♖xc6 bxc6 2.♕d4 with mate to follow

679 – 1.♗f6!! ♗xf6 2.d8♕+

680 – 1.♗d7!! ♕xd7 2.♕h6+ [2.♕g7+ ♔e8 3.♕g8#]

681 – 1.♘g4! fxg4 [1...gxf4 2.♘f6+] 2.♗xc7

682 – 1.♕xa8! ♖f8 [1...♖xa8 2.♖d8+ ♖xd8

3.♖xd8#] 2.♖d8 with a winning position

683 – 1.♕g6! ♕xg6 [1...♖xh7 2.♕e8+] 2.♖h8+ with mate to follow

684 – 1.b4 ♗c7 2.b5+ winning the ♖

685 – 1.♖xf6! gxf6 2.♕g4+ ♔f8 3.♕xd7 with a decisive advantage

686 – 1.♖xd7+! decoy sacrifice 1...♔xd7 2.♖a7+ winning the ♕

687 – 1.♘e7+! ♖xe7 [1...♔f8 2.♘xc6] 2.♖d8#

688 – 1.♘c6 ♕c8 2.♖xd5

689 – 1.♕a3+ ♔g8 [1...♕e7 2.♗xc6! ♕xa3 3.♖xe8#] 2.♗xh7+ winning the ♕

690 – 1.♘f6+ ♖xf6 [1...♔h8 2.♕h7#] 2.♕xe8+

Mixed motifs: Black page 93

691 – 1...♖xd1+! 2.♖xd1 ♕xc3 winning a piece

692 – 1...♕xh2+ 2.♖xh2 ♖g1#

693 – 1...♖xd1+ removing the defender 2.♕xd1 ♕f2#

694 – 1...♕h2#

695 – 1...♗c4#

696 – 1...♖ff1 2.b3 ♖g2+

697 – 1...♖g2+ 2.♔h3 ♖h1#

698 – 1...♖b7+! the only way to prevent mate 2.axb7 stalemate [2.♔a5 ♖b2 theoretical draw]

699 – 1...♖e8 and mate on e1 the next move

700 – 1...♕g4+ 2.♔h1 ♕f3+ 3.♔g1 ♕g4+

701 – 1...♖c1+ 2.♔b2 ♖c2+ 3.♔b1 ♖c1+ 4.♔xc1 stalemate

702 – 1...♖xf4! 2.♖xf4 g5 with an extra piece

703 – 1...♕h1+ 2.♔xh1 ♖xf1#

704 – 1...♖xe3! 2.♕xe3 ♗xd4 winning the ♕

705 – 1...♕h1+! 2.♔xh1 ♖f1#

706 – 1...♖h1+ 2.♔xh1 ♕h4+ 3.♔g1 ♕h2#

707 – 1...♖g1+ 2.♔xg1 ♘h3+

708 – 1...♗c5 winning the ♕

709 – 1...♖a8 the ♗ is pinned, and if it moves, White will be checkmated

710 – 1...♖xf1+ 2.♔xf1 ♕h1#

711 – 1...♔h8! 2.fxg5 ♘g8 winning the ♕

712 – 1...♖e1+ 2.♕xe1 [2.♘xe1 ♕h1#] 2...♕xg2#

713 – 1...♖g1+ 2.♖xg1 ♘f2# Cochrane-Staunton 1841 0-1

714 – 1...♗h3! 2.♕xg5 ♖f1#

715 – 1...♖b2 with 2...♖a2# to follow, Shabalov-Granda Zuniga 2005 0-1

716 – 1...♖xe3+ 2.♖xe3 ♕h6+ winning the ♖

717 – 1...♗e7+ 2.♔h5 ♖h3# McDonnel-De Labourdonnais 1834 0-1

718 – 1...♕xh2+! 2.♔f1 ♕xf2#

719 – 1...d3 controlling e2 with ♕h1 mate to follow

720 – 1...♖a1+! 2.♗xa1 ♖xa1#

721 – 1...♕xd2+ 2.♖xd2 ♖f1+ 3.♔e1 ♖xe1+ 4.♖d1 ♖dxd1#

722 – 1...♘h3+ 2.♔h1 ♗d5#

723 – 1...♗f1+! 2.♕xf1 ♕g3#

724 – 1...♕f3+ 2.♖xf3 ♖b1+ and checkmate follows

725 – 1...♖xf2! 2.♔xf2 [2.♕xf2 ♗c5] 2...♗c5+

726 – 1...♖e2+!! 2.♘xe2 ♘e4+ 3.♔d1 ♘f2#

727 – 1...♕h3+! 2.♔xh3 ♗f1+ 3.♔h4 f5#

728 – 1...♖xh3+! 2.gxh3 g2+ 3.♔xg2 ♕g3+ 4.♔h1 ♕xh3# Leko-Blatny 1991

729 – 1...♕a5+ 2.♗a4 ♕xa4+ 3.bxa4 ♖a3#

730 – 1...♕xb1! 2.♗xb1 ♖e2 Gudmundsson-Fischer 1960 0-1 3.♗c1 ♖e1 winning the ♗, with a decisive advantage

731 – 1...♗xf2+ 2.♕xf2 [2.♔xf2 ♘xe4+] 2...♘d3+ and wins

732 – 1...♖d8! the white ♕ can not leave the diagonal 2.♕xf5 ♖xd1#

733 – 1...♘f5! simple... once you've seen it! 2.♘xf5 ♖xg2+ intermediate check 3.♔c3 ♗xf5

734 – 1...♗h3! 2.♖e1 [2.♘xh3 ♘e2+] 2...♗g2 3.exd4 exd4 4.♕c2 ♖xh1 Black wins

735 – 1...♗g2+ 2.♖xg2 ♕f1+ 3.♖g1 ♘g3+ 4.hxg3 ♕h3#

736 – 1...♕xh2+ 2.♔xh2 ♘g4+ 3.♔g1 ♘h3+ 4.♔f1 ♘h2# Maczinsky-Pratten 1948

737 – 1...♖xa7! it can be captured! 2.♖h7+ ♔e6 3.♖xa7 Stalemate, Anand-Ivanchuk 2004

738 – 1...♕c6!! [1...♖d1+? 2.♖f1] 2.♕xc6 ♖d1+ 3.♖f1 ♖xf1#

739 – 1...♘f3+ 2.exf3 ♕xf1+ Torre-Timman 1982 0-1 3.♔xf1 ♗h3+ 4.♔g1 ♖e1#

740 – 1...♗e2+ 2.♔g2 [2.♔e4?? ♗g4+ 3.♔d4 ♗xd7] 2...♗f1+ 3.♔f3 [3.♔g1?? ♗h3#] 3...♗e2+ draw, Chuchelov-Kritz 2003

741 – 1...♖xa3+! 2.♔xa3 ♕c5+! 3.♔a2 ♕a7#

742 – 1...♖f1+ 2.♔xf1 [2.♔h2 ♕h1#] 2...♕h1+ 3.♔f2 ♘g4# Bogoljubow-Monticelli 1930

743 – 1...♕d1+! 2.♔xd1 ♘e3+ 3.♔e1 ♖d1# Chistiakov-Kogan 1933

744 – 1...♖e1+ 2.♔g2 ♘h4+ 3.♔h2 ♘f3+ draw, Erenburg-Golod 2005

745 – 1...Qd1+!! 2.Rxd1 Nc2+ 3.Nxc2 Rxd1#

746 – 1...Rg3!! Reggio–Mieses 1903 2.Qxg3 [2.hxg3 Qe3+ 3.Be2 Qxe2#] 2...Qh4! this is the idea: to deflect the Q from the third rank 3.Bxa6 [3.Qxh4 Qe3+ 4.Be2 Qxe2#] 3...Bxg3+ 4.hxg3 Qxa6, with a decisive advantage for Black

747 – 1...Rxa3!! The back rank! Mikenas–Bronstein 1965 0–1 [1...Qe1+? 2.Qf1] 2.Qxa3 [2.bxa3 Qa1+ 3.Rb1 Re1+ 4.Rxe1 Qxe1+ 5.Qf1 Qxf1#; 2.Qd1 Rxa1 3.Qxa1 Qe1+; 2.Rxa3 Qe1+ 3.Qf1 Qxf1#] 2...Qe1+ 3.Rxe1 Rxe1#

748 – 1...Rb6+ 2.g6 Rxg6+! 3.Kxg6 stalemate, Kramnik–Grischuk 2005

749 – 1...Rxc4! 2.Qxc4 Qf2+ 3.Kh2 Qh4+ perpetual check, Leko–Kramnik 2004

750 – 1...Kh6! and mate is inevitable! 2.g3 [2.Rcxd3 g5#] 2...g5+ 3.Kh3 Nf4# Rodgaard–Nunn 1988

751 – 1...Qxh3! 2.gxh3 Nf2+ 3.Kg1 Nxh3# Torres–Alekhine 1922

752 – 1...Rxd6! 2.Qxd6 [2.exd6 Qe1+] 2...Rd8! 3.Qxe7 Rd1#

753 – 1...Qh1+!! 2.Kxh1 Bf3+ 3.Kh2 Rh1# Thierring–Schlechter 1900

754 – 1...Rh4! Aaron–Gligoric 1962 0–1 2.Qg2 [2.Qxh4 Qxg1+ 3.Bd1 Qxd1#] 2...Qxg2 3.Rxg2 Rh1+ and wins

755 – 1...b3 2.cxb3 Kxb3#

756 – 1...f3!! with two threats 2.hxg5 [2.exf3 Qe3#] 2...f2#

757 – 1...Qxc3+! 2.bxc3 Ba3# Macdonell–Boden 1869

758 – 1....Re2!! simple and elegant: threatening mate on h2. Znosko-Borovsky–Duras 1909 2.Rxe2 Qxf1#

759 – 1...Qa6! [1...Qb5? 2.Qxe6+ Kh8 3.Qxg6 White wins] 2.Qxg6 Qxe2 and wins

760 – 1...Rh1+!! 2.Rxh1 Kg3 and mate on e1 is unstoppable! Donner–Spanjard 1961 0–1

761 – 1...Rd1+ 2.Nxd1 [2.Ke2 Nd4#] 2...Qc4#

762 – 1...Qg2+!! 2.Rxg2 [2.Rxg2 Nh3#] 2...Ne2#

763 – 1...Re3! 2.Nxe3 Qxd3+ Tukmakov–Gufeld 1972 0–1

764 – 1...Rf5+! Beliavsky–Babula 2005 1/21/2 [1...Re4+?? 2.Kf5 and after 2Re5+the king reach d8 via g6–h7–g8–f7–e6–d7–e8, and

after Rd8+ White retakes the pawn with check] 2.Ke3 Re5+ 3.Kd4 Rd5+ 4.Ke3 Re5+ 5.Kf2 Rf5+ 6.Kg1 Rf1+ 7.Kh2 Rh1+ 68.Kxh1 stalemate

765 – 1...Rxf1+ 2.Kxf1 [2.Rxf1 Qxh2#] 2...Qf2#

766 – 1...Nb3 2.Rh1 Ra1#

767 – 1...Bf3+ 2.Kxf3 Be5! and mate on h2

768 – 1...Rxc3 Aaron–Fischer 1962 0–1 2.bxc3 Qb1+ and checkmate follows

769 – 1...Bf2+ 2.Kxf2 Qc1#

770 – 1...Qxe4! saving the N on d4 and winning the exchange: the N on g3 is overloaded with the twin duties of defending e4 and preventing the fork on e2 2.Qxe4 [2.Bxd4 Qxd4] 2...Ne2+ 3.Kh2 Nxc3 with a decisive advantage

771 – 1...Qxg3+ 2.hxg3 Rh1#

772 – 1...Qxg5!! 2.fxg5 Bf3 and mate cannot be prevented on h1

773 – 1...Nb3+ 2.Bxb3 [2.Kb1 Ned2#] 2...Qa1#

774 – 1...Rxf2+! 2.Kxf2 Qxe3+ 3.Kf1 [3.Kxe3 stalemate] 3...Qc1+ 4.Kg2 Qd2+ 5.Kf3 Qe3+ perpetual check

775 – 1...Rb3!! Maric–Gligoric 1962 0–1 2.axb3 [2.Qxa5 Rxb1+ and mate to follow; 2.Qd1 Rxb1 3.Qxb1 Qxf5 winning] 2...Qxd2

776 – 1...Nb4! 2.cxb4 [2.Qxg2 Nxa2#] 2...Qxb7

777 – 1...Nb3+!! (to deflect the P on a2) 2.axb3 Nc5 the b3 square cannot be defended, and – surprisingly – White can't parry the double threat of mate and the capture of Q, Magalotti–Pantaleoni 1981 0–1 2.Qxg7 [2.Nfe4 Nxb3+ 3.Kc2 Nxd4+] 2...Nxb3#

778 – 1...Qf2+! 2.Kxf2 Rd1+ [2...Rd2+?? 3.Ke1] 3.Ke3 Bxe3#

779 – 1...Ba4! 2.Bd3 [2.axb4 Qc2#] 2...Bxd3

780 – 1...Qf3+! 2.Rxf3 gxf3+ 3.Kxf3 Kf7 4.Ke4 Kxe7 and Black wins

781 – 1...Be5 the White Q has no squares available 2.Qxe5 [2.Qh4 Nf3+] 2...Nf3+

782 – 1...f5+! [1...f1Q 2.Rf6+] 2.Kxh3 [2.Kxf5 f1Q+; 2.gxf6 f1Q] 2...f1Q+ 3.Kh4 Qh1+ 4.Kg3 Qe1+ 5.Kf4 Qf2#

783 – 1...Qb6!! attacking b2 and e3 2.Bxb6 Ne2#

784 – 1...Rd8! 2.Qe3 Qxc2! and the threat of Rd1 is decisive Barcza–Tal 1971 0–1

785 – 1...Qe5!! attacking the Q, the N and

threatening a fork on d3! 2.♖d1 [2.♕xe5 ♘d3+ 3.♔b1 ♖xc1#; 2.♖c4 ♘d3+ 3.♔b1 ♕xd4 4.♖xd4 ♖c1#] 2...♕xg3 and wins

786 – 1...♖xd4! 2.♖xd4 ♖c1+ 3.♔g1 ♖xg1+ 4.♔xg1 ♗c5 and wins

787 – 1...♖d3! threatening mate 2.♘xd3 ♗e6#

788 – 1...♘c3 with mate on the way on d1 Agrest–Kharlov 1993 0–1

789 – 1...♖h1+ 2.♔xh1 ♕h4+ 3.♔g2 ♕xf2+ 4.♔h1 [4.♔h3 ♕g3#] 4...♕h4+ 5.♔g2 ♕g3+ 6.♔h1 ♕h3#

790 – 1...♕e4! [1...d5 2.♕e1!] 2.♕c8+ [2.♕xe4 ♖f1+ 3.♔xf1 ♖xf1#] 2...♔g7 3.h3 ♖f1+ 4.♔xf1 ♖xf1+ 5.♔h2 ♕xd3 and wins

791– 1...♘f3+ 2.gxf3 ♖g5+ 3.♔h1 [3.♔f1 ♕h3+ 4.♔e2 ♖e5#] 3...♕xf2 4.♖g1 ♕xf3+ 5.♖g2 ♕xg2#

792 – 1...♖a7!! the ♖ on b7 is pinned! [1...g5 2.♖b8 g4 3.♖db7 and White wins] 2.♖f7 [2.♖xh7?! b1♕∓] 2...♔h6! Reshevsky–Bole-slavsky 1953 ½–½ [2...b1♕?! 3.♖xf8+ ♔xf8 4.♖xb1 with correct play, a draw; however, Black must still suffer] 3.♖fe7 ♗f8 [3...b1♕?? 4.♖e8+ breaking the pin on the other ♖ 4...♗f8 5.♖xb1] 4.♖f7 ♗h6 5.♖fd7 ♗f8! draw

793 – 1...♖xh2+! 2.♔xh2 ♕f2+ 3.♖g2 ♖h8+ 4.♖h5 ♖xh5+ and wins

794 – 1...♕xg3! 2.♘c6+ [2.fxg3 ♘f3#] 2...♗xc6 3.fxg3 ♘f3+ 4.♔f1 ♗b5#

795 – 1...♗xf2+! White probably thought he was winning, but the undefended ♖ puts that idea to rest 2.♔d2 [2.♗xf2 ♕xc1+] 2...♗xe3+ 3.♔xe3 ♕xe3+ 4.♔xe3 ♘c6 and Black wins

796 – 1...♕g1+ 2.♖xg1 [2.♖xg1 ♘f2#] 2...♖bxg2+ more elegant than the alternative mate [2...♖gxg2+ 3.♔h1 ♖xh2+ 4.♔g1 ♖bg2#] 3.♔h1 ♖g1+ 4.♖xg1 ♘f2#

797 – 1...♖xh4! Faarbod–Panno 1962 0–1 2.♔g2 [2.♘xh4 ♖xf2#; 2.♘e4 dxe4] 2...♘f4+ 3.♔f1 ♕h1+ 4.♘g1 ♖g2#

798 – 1...♘xg3+ 2.hxg3 ♕h6+ 3.♗h3 ♕xh3#

799 – 1...♖h1+ 2.♔g3 ♖g1+ 3.♔h2 ♖h1+ draw

800 – 1...♕g2+ 2.♔xg2 ♘f4+ 3.♔g1 ♘h3#

801 – 1...♕f6! breaking the pin on the ♘, with threats to the ♖ and ♕, Zhu Chen–Kortchnoi 2000 0–1 2.♖h3 ♘f3+ 3.♖xf3 ♕xb2 and wins

802 – 1...♘c7! and both ♗ and ♘ are threatened

803 – 1...♕a1+ 2.♔xa1 ♗d4+ 3.♔b1 ♖a1#

804 – 1...♘e3 2.fxe3 ♕h4+ 3.g3 ♕xg3#

805 – 1...♗xe4! 2.♕xe4 [2.♖xe4 ♕f1+ 3.♕xf1 ♖xf1#; 2.♕d1 ♗xg2#] 2...♕f1+ 3.♕xf1 ♖xf1#

806 – 1...♕xh2+! 2.♔xh2 ♔f7! Neiksans-Stefansson 2004 0–1, 3 ...♖h8 is inevitable, with mate to follow

807 – 1...♖h8!! Mackroth–Flear 0–1 2.♕xh8 ♗g5+ Black can invert the two moves 3.f4 ♗h6; the pawn on h2 will promote

808 – 1...♕d3+!! 2.♔xd3 ♗xc6+ 3.♔e2 ♗xa4 with an extra piece

809 – 1...♕g6! the ♕ must protect e4, d1 and itself, Xhu Chen–Spassky 1999 0–1 2.♕xg6 ♖xd1+ intermediate check 3.♔h2 fxg6

810 – 1...♕g1+!! 2.♖xg1 ♘f2+ 3.♔g2 ♗h3#

811 – 1...♘e3+! fxe3 [2.♗xe3 ♗f3#] 2...♕f5+! 3.♗xf5 exf5#

812 – 1...♖b1+ 2.♖xb1 ♘c2#

813 – 1...♕xg2+!! 2.♔xg2 ♖g6+ 3.♔f3 [3.♔h1 ♘xf2#] 3...♘d2#

814 – 1...♕xc2+ 2.♔xc2 ♗xe4+ 3.♔d2 [3.♔b3 ♗c2#] 3...♖c2#

815 – 1...♘f3+! Kortchnoi–Karpov 1978 0–1 2.gxf3 [2.♔h1 ♘f2#] 2...♖g6+ 3.♔h1 ♘f2#

816 – 1...♗d8! 2.♖d7 ♖xd4! 3.♖xd4 ♗b6 and wins Szabo–Karsa 1978

817 – 1...♖xd6! [1...♘f3+? 2.gxf3 ♗f1+ 3.♖g2] 2.♖xd6 ♖f3+! 3.gxf3 ♗f1#

818 – 1...♘a4!! White may have been expecting perpetual check with ♘b5–c3, but this lovely move, which controls b2 and attacks the ♕, wins immediately 2.♔a2 [2.♔xa4 ♖a1#; 2.♕xa6 ♖a1#; 2.bxa4 ♖xb6] 2...♘xb6 3.♔xb1 and Black wins

819 – 1...♖g2!! deflection and a pin Levy–Garcia 1971 0–1 [1...h6? 2.♖xd3] 2.♖xg2 [2.♖xd3 ♖xf2+] 2...♖xa3 and Black wins

820 – 1...♕e2!! 2.♖xe2 [2.♗xf2 ♕xf2+ 3.♔h1 ♕xe1#; 2.♕c1 ♖xg2+ 3.♔h1 ♖xh2+ 4.♔g1 ♕g2#] 2...♖f1#

821 – 1...♘c4! preventing escape on d2 with mate to follow on a1 or b2

822 – 1...♖xc2+ 2.♔xc2 ♕c3#

823 – 1...♗h4 2.♕xh4 [2.♕f3 ♘f2+] 2...♘xe3#

824 – 1...♕h3! 2.♖xe2 ♕xf1#

825 – 1...♕g3+!! 2.♔xg3 hxg3# [or 2...♗xg3#]

826 – 1...♘h4! with mate on the way Vera-

Nataf 2003 0-1 37.♖f2 ♖8g2+ 38.♖xg2 ♘f3#

827 – 1...♕xh2+ 2.♔xh2 hxg3#

828 – 1...♖e2!! Bagirov-Kholmov 1961 0-1 attacking c3 and f2 2.♖xe2 [2.♕xf6 ♖xe1+ check and then capture on f6?] 2...♕xc3 and wins

829 – 1...♕c4+! 2.♘xc4 bxc4#

830 – 1...♖c1+ 2.♔h2 ♘xg4+ 3.♔g3 ♖g1#

831 – 1...♕d6! deflecting the ♕ from the defence of the e1 square 2.hxg4 [2.♕xd6 ♖xe1#; 2.♖xe8+ ♖xe8 3.♗d2 ♕h2+ 4.♔f1 ♕h1#] 2...♕xb4 and wins

832 – 1...♖xg2 [1...♕f1+? 2.♕g1 ♖xg2 3.♕xf1] 2.♖xg2 ♕f1+ 3.♕g1 ♗xg2#

833 – 1...♖c5!! 2.♖xc5 [2.dxc5 ♕d1#; 2.♖xd7 ♖c1#] 2...♕xb7 and wins

834 – 1...♕g1+ 2.♖xg1 ♘f2#

835 – 1...♔g7! and mate is inevitable, Macieja-Fontaine 2003 0-1 [35...♔xg6?? 36.♘f4+ and wins; 35...fxg6 36.♕c7+ perpetual check]

836 – 1...♗h3+ 2.♔xh3 [2.♔f3 ♕g4#; 2.♔g1 ♕f1#] 2...♕f1#

837 – 1...♖f8 2.♖d8 ♕h4+ capturing the pinned ♕f6, Makogonov-Chekhover 1937 0-1

838 – 1...♘f2+ 2.♖xf2 ♕xa1+ 3.♖f1 ♕xf1#

839 – 1...♕c6+! 2.♕xc6 [2.♔c3 ♕xb7] 2...♘b3#

840 – 1...♕d2+! 2.♔b1 [2.♖xd2 ♖xd2+ 3.♔b1 ♖xb2#] 2...♖xb2+ 3.♖xb2 ♖d1+ 4.♔c2 ♖d2+ 5.♔b1 ♖xb2#

841 – 1...♕g2+ 2.♖xg2 ♘h3#

842 – 1...♕e2! Shkuran-Ivanchuk 2004 0-1 [1...♗xf2+? 2.♔h1 is less effective] 2.♖xe1 ♕xf2+ 3.♔h1 ♕g1#

843 – 1...♘g3+ 2.fxg3 ♕e1#

844 – 1...♖f2+ 2.♗xf2 [2.♔g1 ♖f1+ 3.♔g2?? ♕f3+ 4.♔h2 ♖h1#] 2...♕xf2+ 3.♔h1 ♕f1+

845 – 1...♕d1+! [1...♕f1+?? 2.♕g1 and wins] 2.♕g1 ♕h5+ 3.♖h2 ♕f3+ 4.♕g2 ♕d1+ with perpetual check, Topalov-Motylev 2003

846 – 1...♕d3+! [1...♕b1+?? 2.♔e2 ♕c2+ 3.♔f1 ♕f5+ 4.♔g1 ♕g6+ 5.♔f2 ♕f5+ 6.♕f4] 2.♔c1 ♕c3+ 3.♔d1 ♕d3+ draw

847 – 1...♖xc3+ 2.bxc3 ♗a3+ 3.♔c2 ♗f5#

848 – 1...♖xc3! 2.bxc3 ♖f6+ 3.♔g2 ♕f1+ 4.♔h2 ♖f2+ 5.♖xf2 ♕xf2+ 6.♔h3 ♕f1+ draw

849 – 1...♕xf2+!! 2.♔xf2 [2.♔h3 ♕f1+ 3.♔h2 ♖e2#] 2...♖e2+ 3.♔g1 ♖e1+ 4.♔h2 ♖8e2+ 5.♔h3 ♖h1#

850 – 1...♘h3+ 2.♔g2 ♖f2+ 3.♔g3 ♖f3+ 4.♔g2

♖f2+ 5.♔h1 ♖f1+ draw

851 – 1...♖e1+ 2.♔h2 ♖h1+! 3.♔xh1 ♖e1+ 4.♔h2 ♖h1+! 5.♔xh1 stalemate, Kuzubov-Graf 2005

852 – 1...♔e6! a mating net forms: the ♔ protects d5 and prepares for ♗f8 2.♘c3 ♗f8+ 3.♔c6 ♖b6+ 4.♔xc7 ♗d6+ 5.♔c8 ♖b8#

853 – 1...♘g3+ Shaoteng-Wenjin 2003 0-1 2.hxg3 hxg3 strangely, White can do nothing about the checks on h6/h4 or c1 if the ♗ moves. 3.♗d4 ♕h6+ 4.♔g1 ♕c1#

854 – 1...♕xg2+ 2.♔xg2 ♘g4# Donaldson-Wang 2002

855 – 1...♖xh2+! 2.♔xh2 [2.♖xh2 ♕xc6+] 2...♕xg3+ 3.♔h1 ♕g1#

856 – 1...♖b2+ 2.♖d2 [2.♔f1 ♕f3+ 3.♔g1 ♕g2#] 2...♕d1!! 3.♖xb2 ♕xd8 and wins

857 – 1...♘f2+!! 2.♔xf2 ♖b1+ 3.♗g1 ♖xg1+! Cerda-Fiorito 2003 0-1 4.♔xg1 ♕e1#

858 – 1...♔h6! protecting h5 with the threat of g4+ and ♕f6 # (Lujan-Morovic 2003 0-1) 2.♕d4 ♕f1 #

859 – 1...♔f6! and ♕e6 mate is inevitable 2.♗f5 gxf5

860 – 1...♖xh5+! 2.♖xh5 ♔h6! 3.♖xh6 ♔xh6 with the ♔ so far away the ♙ will promote

861 – 1...♗f5! e 2...♖h8 mate cannot be avoided

862 – 1...♖g2+ Diu-Akopian 2002 0-1 2.♗xg2 ♖d1+ 3.♗f1 ♖xf1#

863 – 1...♕xg2+! 2.♔xg2 ♖xe2 the ♕ is pinned and Black remains the exchange up

864 – 1...♕f3!! 2.gxf3 ♖xg1 and mate on g2, Schneider-Roiz 2005 0-1

Mate in three page 109

865 – 1.♕c8+ ♔b8 2.♕c6+!! ♗xc6 3.♗xc6#

866 – 1.♕xh5+!! ♗xh5 2.f7+ discovered check 2...e5 3.♗xe5#

867 – 1.♗d2! controlling a5 1...♖xd4 [1...b5 2.axb5+ cxb5 3.cxb5#] 2.b5+ cxb5 3.axb5#

868 – 1.♖h8+! ♔xh8 2.♕h6+ and we see the idea 2...♔g8 3.♕xg7#

869 – 1.♕e8+! ♔xe8 2.♗b5+ ♔d8 [2...♔f8 3.♖e8#] 3.♖e8#

870 – 1.♕xg7+!! ♘xg7 2.♖h6+ ♔g8 3.♘e7#

871 – 1.♘e6+!! ♕xe6 [1...fxe6 2.♕f8#; 1...♔g8 2.♕b8+ ♕d8 3.♕xd8#] 2.♕h6+! ♔xh6 [2...♔g8 3.♕f8#] 3.♗f8#

872 – 1.Qg7+!! Rxg7 2.Nh6+ Kh8 3.fxg7#

873 – 1.Qf8+! Rxf8 2.Rxf8+ Kd7 3.e6#

874 – 1.Nb6+! cxb6 [1...Kb8 2.Rd8#] 2.c7+ Nd5 3.Bxd5#

875 – 1.Ne4! the threat of Nf6 is lethal 1...f5 [1...Qxg3 2.Nf6#] 2.Qxg6+ Kf7 3.Qg7#

876 –1.Qxc6+! bxc6 2.Bxa6+ Qb7 3.Nxe7#

877 – 1.Nxg7+ Kd8 2.Nf6+! Nxf6 3.Be7#
Anderssen–Kieseritsky London 1851

878 – 1.Qa6+! problem by Stamma 1...Nxa6 [1...Kb8 2.Qxb7#] 2.Bxb7+ Kb8 3.Nc6#

879 – 1.Rg5+! Kxg5 [1...Kh6 2.Nf7#] 2.Nf7+ Kh5 3.g4#

880 – 1.Nh5+!! Rxh5 2.Rxg6+! Kxg6 3.Re6#
study by Abu Naim, from around the year 800!

881 – 1.Ng4+!! a problem by Stamma from the 18th century... perhaps too similar to the previous study by Abu Naim! 1...Rxg4 2.Rf5+ Kxf5 3.Rd5#

882 – 1.Nh6! Rf8 2.Ng8+ Rxg8 3.Nxf7#

883 – 1.Qe6!! The R on a6 and the B on c8 control h6 and h3 respectively. No matter how Black recaptures on e6 the capturing piece will interfere with the action of its companion. 1...Bxe6 [1...Rxe6 2.Nhg6+ Kg8 3.Rh8#] 2.Nf5+ Kg8 3.Ne7#

884 – 1.Qg6+!! Bxg6 2.Ng5+! hxg5 3.hxg6# discovered and double check

885 – 1.Qh6! Bxf6 [1...Bxh6 2.Ne7#] 2.Nxf6+ Kh8 3.Qxh7#

886 – 1.Kf5 threatening mate on g6. Without the presence of the P, it would be a theoretical draw 1...Rg7 2.Rh8+ Rh7 3.Rxh7#

887 – 1.Rxd5+ cxd5 2.Ng6+ hxg6 3.f4#

888 – 1.Nh5+ gxh5 2.Qg5+ Kf8 3.Rd8#

889 – 1.Qxh7+! [the same mate follows 1.Nxf7+ Nxf7 2.Qxh7+! Nxh7 3.Ng6#] 1...Nxh7 2.Nxf7+! Nxf7 3.Ng6#

890 – 1.g4+! fxg3 2.Qg2! g4 3.Nf4#

891 – 1.Bb6+!! Kxb6 2.c8N+ Ka5 3.b4# Lolli 18th century

892 – 1.Rc6+!! Bxc6 2.Nc5+ Ka5 3.Bc7#

893 – 1.Qh8+!! elegant and strong 1...Kxh8 2.Bf6+ Kg8 3.Rd8#

894 – 1.Rg1+ Kh6 2.Rd2 [otherwise 2.Rd3] 2...Rad8 3.Rh2#

895 – 1.Bb6!! Bf4 [1...Bxb6 2.Kxb6 e1=Q 3.c7#] 2.c7+ Kxc7 3.Ba7#

896 – 1.Ra8+! Kxa8 2.Qa6+ Kb8 3.Qxb7#

897 – 1.Rf8+! Qxf8 2.Rxf8+ Rxf8 3.Qxg6#

898 – 1.Rxb6+! Qxc6 2.Rxa2+

899 – 1.Rxf7+! Rxf7 2.Nf6+ Kh8 3.Rg8#

900 – 1.Qxh6+!! Kxh6 [1...gxh6 2.Rxh8#] 2.Rxh8+ Kg5 3.Rh5#

901 – 1.Rh8+ Kf7 2.Qxg7+! Kxg7 3.R1h7#

902 –1.Qc6!! threatens mate and pins the B 1...Bxc6 [1...bxa5 2.Rd8+ Qc8 3.Rxc8#; 1...Rg7 2.Rd8+ Qc8 3.Rxc8#] 2.Rd8+ Qc8 3.Rxc8#

903 – 1.Qxd8+! Kxd8 2.Bf6+ Ke8 3.Rc8#

904 – 1.Qxh8+! Kxh8 2.Bf6+ Kg8 3.Re8#

905 – 1.Bg7+! Kg8 [1...Bxg7 2.Rxe8+ Bf8 3.Rxf8#] 2.Bd5+ Re6 3.Bxe6#

906 – 1.Qa8+ Kh7 2.Qh8+! Nxh8 3.Rg7#

907 – 1.Qxc5+! Stamma 1...dxc5 [1...Nb5 2.Nc4#] 2.Nc4+ Kb5 3.Rb6#

908 – 1.Qg7+! Rxg7 2.Qh6+ Rh7 3.Qxh7#

909 – 1.h4+ Kh5 2.Rf5+! gxf5 3.Bf7#

910 – 1.g4+! hxg3 2.e4+ Kf4 3.Rf6#

911 – 1.Re5! b4 [1...Kh3 2.Re4 Kxh2 3.Rh4#] 2.Kg2 b3 3.h3#

912 – 1.Rxf8+! Bxf8 2.Qf7+ Kh8 3.Qxf8#

913 – 1.Qf6+! Bxf6 2.gxf6+ Kf8 3.Rxh8#

914 – 1.Qxf8+ Rxf8 2.Bh6+ Kg8 3.Re8#

915 – 1.Rf4+ Kh5 2.g3! Rhf8 3.Rh4#

916 – 1.Qxh7+! Kxh7 2.Rh3+ Kg8 3.Nxe7#

917 – 1.Rxe8+! Rxe8 2.Rg7+ Kf8 [2...Kh8 3.Nf7#] 3.Nd7#

918 – 1.Qxh6+! gxh6 2.Rg8+ Rxg8 3.Nxf7#

919 – 1.Bg7+! Kf7 2.Qe6+! Nxe6 3.dxe6#

920 – 1.Qxg8+!! Kxg8 [1...Ke7 2.Qe8#] 2.Rh8+! Kxh8 3.Bf7#

921 – 1.Qxf6! gxf6 2.Rg1+ Kh8 3.Bxf6#

922 – 1.Qxf8+! Kxf8 2.Rd8+ Ke7 3.Re8#

923 – 1.Qg4+!! Bxg4 2.Rxh6+ gxh6 3.Bf7#

924 – 1.Qa8+ Qa7 2.Rxb6+!! Bxb6 [2...Kxb6 3.Qc6+] 3.Bc4#

925 – 1.Qg7+!! Kxg7 2.Nf5+ Kg8 3.Nh6#

926 – 1.Qf8+ Kd7 2.Be6+! Kxe6 3.Qf5#

927 – 1.Qe6+!! fxe6 2.Bh5+ g6 3.Bxg6#

928 – 1.Qxh7+!! Nxh7 2.Bxh7+ Kh8 3.Ng6#

929 – 1.Rg8+!! Rxg8 [1...Kxg8 2.Bf6+ Rg7 3.Rd8#] 2.Rg1+ Kh8 3.Bf6#

930 – 1.Na6+!! Rxd8 2.Qb8+! Rxb8 3.Nc7#

931 – 1.Ra8+! Kxa8 2.Nd7!! Re7 3.Na4#

932 – 1.Qg8+!! Rxg8 2.Nxg6+ hxg6 3.Rh4#

933 – 1.Nc7+ Kf8 2.Qd8+! Rxd8 3.Re8#

934 – 1.Qxd6+!! Kxd6 2.Bf4+ Kd7 3.Be6#

Solutions

935 – 1.Rc8+!! Qxc8 2.Qxg7+ Rxg7 3.Rxg7#
936 – 1.Qh6+!! Rxh6 2.Bxh6+ Kh7 3.Rf8#
937 – 1.Qxd8+!! Rxd8 2.gxf7+ Ke7 3.Rc5#
938 – 1.Ne6!! Rxf7 [1...Qxh4 2.Bg7#] 2.g5+ Qxg5+ 3.Qxg5#
939 – 1.Qxh6+ gxh6 2.Rxh6+ Rh7 3.Rxf6#
940 – 1.Qxg7+! Kxg7 2.Rg4+ Kh8 3.Bf6#
941 – 1.Qg5!! Rg8 2.Qxh6+ gxh6 3.Rxg8#
942 – 1.Qxf7+ Nxf7 2.Bxf7+ Kd8 3.Ne6#
943 – 1.Be7+! [1.Qxh7+? Kxh7 2.Rh1+ Kg6!] 1...Kh8 2.Qxh7+! Kxh7 3.Rh1#
944 – 1.Nf6+! gxf6 [1...Kh8 2.Nf7#] 2.Qf7+ Kh8 3.Qh7#
945 – 1.Qh7+! Kxh7 2.Nf6+ Kh8 3.Ng6#

Mate in four page 117
946 –1.Nf6 Re7 2.Rxe7 Ra7 3.Rxa7 a1Q 4.Rh7#
947 – 1.g8Q+ Kxg8 [1...Nf6 2.Qe6+] 2.Ke6 zugzwang 2...Kh8 3.Kf7 e5 4.Bg7# A famous 1895 study by Troitzky
948 – 1.Nf7+ Kg8 2.Nh6+ Kh8 3.Qg8+ Rxg8 4.Nf7# smothered mate
949 – 1.exf7+ Kf8 2.Re8+ Rxe8 3.Bg7+ Kxg7 4.fxe8Q#
950 – 1.Qe3+ Kh7 2.Qa7+ Kh6 [2...Kh8 3.Qg7#] 3.Qg7+ Kh5 4.Qg5# Martens-Grabchevsky 1968
951 – 1.Qg6+ fxg6 2.Bg8+ Kh8 3.Bf7+ Kh7 4.fxg6# [4.Bxg6#]
952 – 1.Ne7+ Bxe7 2.Rxe6+ Rf7 3.Rxf7+ Kh8 4.Qh5#
953 – 1.Qg8+ Rxg8 2.Nxg6+ Kh7 3.Ne5+ Kh8 4.Nf7#
954 – 1.Bxh7+ Rxh7 2.Rxh7 threatening Qh8 mate 2...Kxh7 3.Qh8+ Kg6 4.Qh5#
955 – 1.Bh6+ Kg8 2.Qg5+!! deflection 2...Qxg5 3.Re8+ Kf8 4.Rxf8#
956 – 1.Rxg7+ Kxg7 2.Rf7+ Kxh6 3.Qxh7+ Kg5 4.Rf5#
957 – 1.b8Q+ Rxb8 2.Bd4+ Kb7 [2...Ka6 3.Ra1+ Kb7 4.Ra7#] 3.Rc7+ Ka6 4.Ra7#
958 –1.Rh3+ Nh6 2.Rxh6+ gxh6 3.g7+ Kh7 4.g6#
959 – 1.Rg1+ Kh3 2.Qh7+ Kh4 3.Qd7+!! deflection 3...Qxd7 [3...Rg4 4.Qxg4#] 4.Rg3#
960 – 1.Rd7!! threatening 2.Qh6 mate 1...Bxd7 2.Qd6+ Ke7 3.Qh6+ Ke8 4.Rg8#
961 – 1.Qg8+ decoy sacrifice 1...Kxg8 [1...Rxg8 2.Nf7#] 2.Ne7+ discovered check

2...Kf8 3.N5g6+ hxg6 4.Nxg6#
962 – 1.Nf6+ Kxf6 2.Rfe1+ Be6 [2...Be7 3.Qd8#] 3.Ra4+! Nxa4 4.Qd7#
963 – 1.Rxh7+ Kxh7 2.Qh3+ Kg7 3.Bh6+ Kh7 [3...Kf7 4.Qe6#] 4.Bf8#
964 – 1.Nxe6+ Ke7 [1...Rxe6 2.Qh8+ Kf7 3.Rxg7#] 2.Rxg7+ Kxe6 3.Qg6+ Kxe5 4.f4# Miles-Jakobsen 1984
965 – 1.Qe8+! Rxe8 [1...Kxe8 interfering with the R's control of the c8 square 2.c7+ Rxf3 3.c8Q#] 2.Rxe8+ Bxe8 3.c7+ Rxf3 4.c8Q# Mieses-Von Bardeleben 1905
966 – 1.Qxh7+ Kxh7 2.Nf6+ double check 2...Kh8 3.Rh3+ Bh4 4.Rxh4#
967 – 1.Nf6+ gxf6 2.Qh7+ Kf8 3.Nxe6+ fxe6 4.Bh6# Medrutchi-Freytag 1935
968 – 1.Rxf7+ Rxf7 2.Nh5+ Kh8 [2...Kg8 3.Qd8+] 3.Qd8+ Rf8 4.Qxf8#
969 – 1.Qxg6+! Kh8 [1...Kxg6 2.Rg3#] 2.Bxf5 removing the defender 2...exf5 [2...Rxf6 3.Qh7#] 3.Qxh6+ Rh7 4.Qxh7#
970 – 1.Rh8+ Bxh8 2.Qh7 threatening mate on g8 2...Kg6 3.Rxh8+ Qg8 4.Qxg8# Martinez-Vaganian Moscow 1975
971 – 1.Bg7+!! decoys and opens a line 1...Kxg7 2.Rxh7+! Kxh7 3.Qxg6+ Kh8 4.Qh7#
972 – 1.f6+ Kg8 [1...Kxf6 2.Qh6+ Kg8 3.Qh7#] 2.Rh8+ Kxh8 3.Qh6+ Kg8 4.Qg7# Marshall-Marco 1900
973 – 1.Qg7+!! Rxg7 2.hxg7+ Kg8 3.Rh8+ Kxf7 4.g8Q#
974 – 1.Qc7+! taking away an escape square! 1...Kxc7 2.Bb6+!! Kb8 [2...axb6 3.Rd8#] 3.Rd8+ Qc8 4.Rxc8# Manka-Braga 1992
975 – 1.Qh7+ Nxh7 2.Nhg6+ Kg8 3.Nxe7+ Kh8 4.N5g6# Majewskaja-Kirjenko 1974
976 – 1.Qh6+! Bxh6 2.Bxh6+ Kh7 3.Bf8+ Qh4 4.Rxh4#
977 –1.Nc7+ Qxc7 2.Qe2+ Qe5 3.Qxe5+ Be7 4.Qxe7#
978 – 1.Qxh6+! gxh6 2.Bd4+ Be5 3.Rxe5+ Rf6 4.Bxf6#

Curiosities page 121
979 –This seems a study, but it is actually from a real game (Kopylov-Karlson 1961, with colours reversed). 1. Rd6!!, 1...Nxd6 2. Be3#, or 1...gxf6 2. Rc6#, or 1...Rc8 2. Nxa6#

980 – Black, with a completely won position, played...d4?? 1.♗c3 and mate on h8 cannot be prevented! Garcia–Ivkov 1965 1–0. Had Ivkov not made this blunder, he would have won the tournament ahead of Smyslov (the tournament winner), Fischer and Geller!

981 – 1...♕a5+ and Black wins the ♗ on g5, Djordievic–Kovacevic 1984 0–1. In subsequent years, other master strength players have made this error eight times ... but on two occasions managing to salvage a draw!

982 – 1.h8♘+! a ♕ or ♖ promotion creates stalemate, whereas a ♗ promotion creates a theoretical draw. Now it is mate in 14 moves with best play!

983 – 1.♔h2! Schlechter–Meitner 1899 1–0, the threat of ♗f2 cannot be met

984 – 1. c1♗.♗h7! as odd looking as it is effective! The idea is to control g8. Hommeles–Skoblikov 1992 1–0. 1...♖xh7 [1...♗xc5 23.♕xc5+ and mate; 1...♗d6 2.♕e8+! ♕xe8 34.♗xd6+ ♕e7 4.♗xe7+ ♔e8 5.♗f5 and wins] 2.♗xe7+ ♔g8 3.♗xd8 ♖xd8 4.♕e8+ ♖xe8 5.♖xe8#

985 – The famous encounter Von Popiel–Marco 1902. Here Black – not seeing any way to save the pinned ♗ – resigned. In fact, he could have won with 1...♗g1!! threatening mate on h2 2.♔xg1 [2.♕xd7 ♕xh2#] 2...♖xd3 3.♗xd3 ♗xe4

986 – Black threatens the ♕ and the ♔; it is impossible to save both! 1.♘d5+ the power of double check 1...♔d8 [1...♔b7 2.♕c7+ ♔a6 3.♕b6#; 1...♔b8 2.♕c7#] 2.♕c7+ ♔e8 3.♕e7#

987 – 1.♖e5!! strange but true: White wins a piece 1...♗xe5 [1...♖dxe5+ 2.dxe5 Black has two pieces hanging] 2.dxe5 The ♔ will win one of the ♖s

988 – 1.♘h7!! Razuvaev–Mestrovic 1981 1–0 1...♖xc8 [1...♔xh7 2.♖xf8] 2.♘xf6+ intermediate check 2...gxf6 3.♖xc8+ and wins

989 – Black has just promoted to a ♘ in order to prevent the fork on f3; remember that 2 ♘s vs. ♔ is a theoretical draw . Now White doesn't seem to have a move, but there is... 1.♘f3+!! ♘xf3+ 2.♔g3 attacking all three ♘s 2...♔e3 the only chance, but now it stalemate! A 1937 study by Kubbel

990 – 1...♕g3!! Other less spectacular moves win too. Wrongly or rightly, many consider this to be the most spectacular tactical move of all time: Levitzky–Marshall 1912. 2.♕xg3 [2.hxg3

♘e2#; 3.fxg3 ♘e2+ 4.♔h1 ♖xf1#] 2...♘e2+ 3.♔h1 ♘xg3+ 4.fxg3 ♖xf1#

991 – Here White accepted a draw offer, but... 1.♖g7!! would have won the game; it threatens ♘f5 mate 1...♔xg7 [1...♕c8 2.♘f5+ ♕xf5 3.gxf5 ♔xg7 4.e4 and wins] 2.♘e6+ ♔f7 3.♘xd8+ with victory

992 – 1.♔g3!! The ♔ is heading to h6 with mate on g7 and there is nothing Black can do about it! 1...♖ce8 2.♔f4 ♗c8 3.♔g5 Short–Timman 1991 1–0

993 – 1.♔g5!! ♗d5 2.♔h6! Weenink–Gans 1936 1–0, and mate g7 is on the way

994 – 1.♕a8! winning a piece: Panczyk–Schurade 1978 1–0 1...♖xa8 [1...♖b7 2.♕xb8 ♖xb8 3.♘xe7+] 2.♘xe7+ ♔h7 3.♘xc8

995 – White has just sacrificed the ♕ on f6 and Black resigned! BUT... 1...♕g4! would have won the game [1...gxf6? 2.♖g3+ ♔h8 3.♗xf6#] 2.hxg4 gxf6 and the g file is not accessible for White, who is simply a ♖ down

996 – Seeing mate on f1 or e1, White threw in the towel, Jonasson–Angantysson 0–1, BUT 1.♘e3! results in f1 being protected by the ♕ [1.♔h1?? exf1♕#] 1...♗xe3+ 2.♔h1 exf1♕+ 3.♕xf1 with a decisive advantage

997 – Faced with the threat of ♕xh3+, White resigned; however, he could have won the game with 1.♖e8+ [1.♖xd4? ♕xe1+] 1...♔d7 2.♖e3!! ♕f4 3.♖xd4+! ♕xd4 4.♖d3 ♕xd3 5.♘e5+

998 – Black has just captured on e1, and White resigned because of 1.♗xe1 ♖e3+ 2.♔d2 ♖xe5, but the intermediate move 1.g6! would have saved the day: the check on g7 is fatal

999 – White resigned at this point in the game Torre–NN played in a simultaneous exhibition in 1924. In fact, Torre could have won by playing 1.♖d6!! [1.f7?? ♖c1+ 2.♔e2 d1♕+] 1...♖xd6 [1...cxd6 now the ♙ on d2 is no longer a threat 2.f7 and wins] 2.g8♕+ ♔d7 [2...♖d8 3.♕xd8+ ♔xd8 4.f7] 3.♕xh7+ ♔c6 4.♕e4+ ♔b6 5.♕b4+ ♔c6 6.♕xc5+ ♔xc5 7.f7 and wins

1000 – 1.♗a7!! with the threat of ♗b6 mate. Steel–NN 1886 1–0

1001 – 1.e4! From a 1935 study by Kasparian. The ♙ not only forks the two ♖s, but also threatens mate on the following move! 1...♖c5 [1...♖g5 2.exd5#] 2.exf5#

Glossary

Tactics

closing lines (a.k.a. interference or obstruction) a tactic that results in the obstruction of a file, rank or diagonal, with short term tactical consequences for the opponent

combination a combination of two or more different tactical motifs in series, often involving a sacrifice

decoy sacrifice a sacrifice that forces the capturing piece to a key square, with negative consequences

deflection a capture or threat forces a piece away from its defence of a piece or a key square

discovery the movement of a piece unmasks a threat by a second piece

double attack (see fork) a single piece threatens two undefended pieces simultaneously.

discovered check the movement of a piece unmasks a check by a second piece

double check the movement of a piece that checks the king unmasks another check from a second piece

double threat the most important single concept in tactics: a move by a single piece creates two problems simultaneously (e.g. threat of mate and unprotected piece capture, threat of mate and pawn promotion, etc.). Most other tactical terms describe specific types of a double threat.

fork a double attack by a pawn or a knight

intermediate move (a.k.a. zwischenzug, intermezzo, or in-between move) an unexpected move by an opponent in a planned tactical sequence

opening lines (a.k.a. clearance) a tactic that results in the opening of a file, rank or diagonal, with short term tactical consequences for the opponent

pin the movement of a piece is impossible or restricted as it is on the same line of attack as the king or a more valuable piece

removing the defender (a.k.a. removing the guard) the capture of a key defending piece, usually involving a sacrifice

sacrifice the capture of a piece by a more valuable piece so as to gain a subsequent tactical or strategic benefit

skewer the movement of a piece under attack would result in the capture of an undefended piece of less value on the same line of attack

windmill a series of repeated discovered checks that result in the capture of several pieces by the piece which unmasks check

Miscellaneous

blockade stopping a pawn's advance by placing (usually) a bishop or knight in front of it

epaulette mate a back rank checkmate made possible because the king's movement is restricted by the presence of a piece of the same colour on each side of the king, usually the rooks

escape square an unoccupied square that an attacked piece can flee to

exchange sacrifice the exchange of a rook for a bishop or knight

the square (a.k.a. the square of the pawn) a simple method for determining if a king can prevent a pawn from promoting. Visualise a square made up of the line between pawn and its promotion square and three other lines of equal length. If an unimpeded king is in that square with the opponent to move, the king can prevent pawn promotion.

hanging piece an undefended piece that is under attack

loose piece an undefended piece that is not under immediate attack

mating net usually quiet moves that trap the king in preparation of mate

Novotny theme this is the term used when a piece is sacrificed on a square where it could be taken by two different opponent pieces – whichever piece makes the capture obstructs the action of the other.

overloaded piece a piece that has more defensive tasks than it can cope with

promotion a pawn reaches the last rank and is substituted by any other piece.

smothered mate a checkmate in which the king cannot move because of the presence of pieces of the same colour on all adjacent squares to the king

stalemate the game is a draw when a player's king is not in check and he can't make a legal move

theoretical draw a known endgame position where a draw is the inevitable result of best play

vacating a square a piece moves with a threat or a sacrificial capture in order to allow access for another piece of the same colour to the square the capturing piece previously occupied

wrong coloured bishop (a.k.a. wrong bishop) a bishop that controls the dark squares in an endgame position where you require a bishop that controls the light squares to win or draw, or vice versa

zugzwang a position that would be sound if you could skip your move, i.e. it is your turn to move, and any move you make will have negative consequences